hampsteadthe

hampsteadtheatre and Thelma Holt
by arrangement with the Royal Shakespeare Company
present

the giant

by Antony Sher

Media sponsor for **The Giant**

Pink Paper 20 07

hampsteadtheatre gratefully acknowledges
the support of

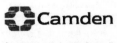

Funded by Camden Council

hampsteadtheatre and Thelma Holt
by arrangement with the Royal Shakespeare Company present

the giant

by **Antony Sher**

Cast

Vito	**Stephen Hagan**
Old Vito	**Richard Moore**
Leonardo Da Vinci	**Roger Allam**
Michelangelo	**John Light**
Machiavelli	**Stephen Noonan**
Lodovico / Soderini	**Philip Voss**
Salai	**Simon Trinder**
Spini	**Mark Meadows**
Pandolfini	**Barry McCarthy**
First Acolyte	**Nick Court**
Second Acolyte	**Ricky Champ**
Contucci / Singer	**Ian Conningham**

Creative Team

Director	**Gregory Doran**
Designer	**William Dudley**
Lighting Designer	**Oliver Fenwick**
Sound Designer	**Matt McKenzie for Autograph**
Composer	**Paul Englishby**
Movement	**Anna Morrissey**
Musical Director	**Mark Meadows**
Costume Supervisor	**Joan Hughes**
Voice/Dialect Coach	**George Richmond-Scott**
Casting Director	**Ginny Schiller**
Assistant Director	**Mel Cook**
Company Stage Manager	**Mike Powell-Jones**
Stage Manager	**Ernie Hall**
Deputy Stage Manager	**Briony Allen**
Wardrobe Maintenance	**Greg Dunn**
Set Built and Painted by	**RSC Workshops**
Construction Manager	**Alan Bartlett**
David sculpted by	**Roger Cresswell**
Press Representative	**Becky Sayer** (020 7449 4151)

hampsteadtheatre would like to thank:
Barry Claydon at Marriott Hotel, Regent's Park

The Giant **was first performed at Hampstead Theatre, London,
on Thursday 1 November 2007**

cast and creative team

Antony Sher (Writer)
Antony Sher is an actor, author and artist. He trained at the Webber Douglas Academy of Dramatic Art. His work at the National includes *Primo* (winner of both New York Outer Critic's Circle and Drama Desk awards as Outstanding Solo Performance), *True West*, *Stanley*, for which he won an Olivier Award for Best Actor, *Uncle Vanya*, *The Resistible Rise of Arturo Ui*, and *Titus Andronicus* (in a co-production with Market Theatre, Johannesburg) for which he won a TMA Best Actor Award. For the RSC: *Othello*, *The Roman Actor*, *The Malcontent*, *Macbeth*, *The Winter's Tale*, *Cyrano de Bergerac*, *Travesties*, *Tamburlaine the Great*, *Singer*, *Hello and Goodbye*, *The Revenger's Tragedy*, *The Merchant of Venice*, *Richard III*, for which he won Olivier and Evening Standard Best Actor awards, *Red Noses*, *Maydays*, *Tartuffe*, *Molière* and *King Lear*; his own play *I.D.* at the Almeida; *Mahler's Conversion* at the Aldwych; *Torch Song Trilogy*, for which he won an Olivier Award for Best Actor, at the Albery; *Goosepimples* at Hampstead and the Garrick, and *Kean* at the Apollo Theatre and tour. Television includes: *Primo*, *Home*, *Macbeth*, *The Jury*, *Genghis Cohen*, *The History Man*. Film includes: *Mrs Brown* (Peter Sellers Evening Standard Film Award), *Shakespeare in Love*, *Alive and Kicking*, *The Young Poisoner's Handbook*. Writing includes: the stage plays *I.D.* and *Primo*; the novels *Middlepost*, *The Indoor Boy*, *Cheap Live*, *The Feast*; the theatre journals *Year of the King*, *Woza Shakespeare!* (co-writtern with Gregory Doran), *Primo Time*; an autobiography *Beside Myself*; the BBC TV film *Changing Step*; the Channel 4 documentary *Murder Most Foul* (co-written with Jon Blair); and a book of his drawings and paintings *Characters*. He has held exhibitions of his paintings and drawings at the Barbican (1985), the National Theatre (1996) and the London Jewish Cultural Centre (2007). He has honorary doctorates from the universities of Liverpool, Exeter and Warwick and is an Associate Artist of the RSC. In 2000 he was knighted for services to acting and writing.

Roger Allam (*Leonardo Da Vinci*)
Roger is an Associate Artist of the RSC where his classical roles include: Mercutio, Oberon/Theseus, Brutus, Toby Belch, Duke Vincentio in *Measure for Measure*, Benedick, Macbeth and Trigorin in *The Seagull*. He also played leading roles in plays by Peter Flannery, Robert Holman, Arthur Miller, Deborah Levy, Trevor Griffiths and David Edgar, and created the role of Javert in *Les Misérables*. For the National Theatre: Willy Brandt in *Democracy*, Lopakhin in *The Cherry Orchard*, Hitler in *Albert Speer*, Bassov in *Summerfolk*, Graves in *Money*, Ulysses in *Troilus and Cressida*, Mirabelle in *The Way of the World*. Other theatre includes: *Aladdin*, *The Importance of Being Earnest* (Old Vic); *Privates on Parade* (Donmar); *City of Angels, Arcadia, Art, Boeing Boeing* (West End); *Pravda* (Chichester Festival Theatre). He has been nominated five times for an Olivier Award-winning twice for *Money* and *Privates on Parade*. He also won the Clarence Derwent Award for *Troilus and Cressida*. Recent television includes: *The Thick of It, A Class Apart,*

Spooks 5, Inspector Lynley, Manchild, Foyle's War, The Creatives. Film includes: *Speed Racer, The Queen, The Wind That Shakes the Barley, V for Vendetta, A Cock and Bull Story, The Roman Spring of Mrs Stone, Stranded.* Radio includes: more than sixty radio plays, most recently *Great Expectations.*

Stephen Hagan (*Vito*)
Stephen graduated from LAMDA in 2007. His work there included *Anna Karenina* directed by Joseph Blatchley, *Others* directed by Hannah Eidinow. Other theatre includes: *Troilus and Cressida* (RSC/EIF); *There Was an Old Woman...* (Lyric Theatre, Belfast). Television: *Clapham Junction* directed by Adrian Shergold for Channel 4.

Ricky Champ (*Second Acolyte*)
Ricky graduated from the Guildhall School of Music and Drama in 2005. His work there included *12 Angry Men, Orestes 2.0, Troilus and Cressida, Corpus Christi, Platanov.* Other theatre includes: *Coriolanus* (RSC); *Bent* (West End). Television includes: *The Bill, Family Affairs.* Film includes: *Driving Lessons, Hotel Very Welcome.*

Nick Court (*First Acolyte*)
Theatre includes: *The Tempest, Julius Caesar, Antony and Cleopatra* (RSC); *A Few Good Me*n (Theatre Royal Haymarket); *Who's Afraid of Virginia Woolf?* (Liverpool Playhouse); *The Elephant Man* (Sincera Productions); *The Shape of Things* (Kenny Wax Products). Television includes: *Between Two Rivers, Silent Witness, The Bill, Jim and The Angel, 55 Degrees North.*

Ian Conningham (*Contucci / Singer in the Masque*)
Ian trained at Rose Bruford College of Speech and Drama. Theatre includes: *Take Flight* (Menier Chocolate Factory); *Merry Wives of Windsor* (RSC); *King Cotton* (Workshop – Lowry Theatre); *Hot Mikado (Watermill); The Lion, the Witch and the Wardrobe, Wind in the Willows* (West Yorkshire Playhouse); *Silver Sword* (Nottingham Playhouse); *Oh! What A Lovely War* (Theatr Clwyd); *The Railway Children* (Saddlers Wells/Peacock Theatre); *The Buddy Holly Story* (Strand Theatre); *Heavy Pencil* (Workshop performance – Menier Chocolate Factory); *Jean De Florette* (The Venue); *Alfie* (Watford Palace); *Sugar* (New Wolsey/Theatre Clwyd); *Return to the Forbidden Planet* (National tour); *Heaven Can Wait* (Belgrade Theatre Coventry/National tour); *Pump Boys and Dinettes, The Jungle Book* (Haymarket Theatre, Basingstoke); *Tutti Frutti* (National tour). Television, film and radio includes: *Courtroom, Brookside, Settling Up, Millions, Post Haste, Going Off Big Time, The Epiphany of Theodocious Pennington,* and various characters for *The Sauce Radio Show.*

Barry McCarthy (*Pandolfini*)
Theatre includes: *Kean* (Apollo Theatre/tour); *The Canterbury Tales, As You Like It, Back to Methuseleh, Wildest Dreams, The Park* (RSC); *The Master and Margarita, King Lear, The Government Inspector, A Midsummer Night's Dream, The Scarlet Letter, The Coffee House, The Merchant of Venice* (Chichester Festival Theatre); *Things We Do For Love* (Gielgud/Scarborough); *Henceforward* (Scarborough/tour). Television includes: *Judge John Deed, Holby City, House of Cards, Peak Practice, Scott of the Arms Antics, The Muscle Market, First and Last.* Film includes: *Notes on a Scandal, Kinky Boots, Food for Love, Brothers and Sisters.*

John Light (*Michelangelo*)
John trained at LAMDA. Theatre includes: *My Boy Jack* (Hampstead Theatre); *Julius Caesar, The Tempest, The Seagull* (nominated for Ian Charleson Award), *In the Company of Men, A Patriot for Me* (RSC); *The Tempest* (Novello Theatre); *The Night Season* (National Theatre); *Singer* (Oxford Stage Company); *Certain Young Men, The Tower* (nominated for Ian Charleson), *The Cenci* (Almeida Theatre); *Clocks and Whistles* (Bush Theatre); *Macbeth* (National Youth Theatre). Television includes: *Dresden, North And South, Dalziel And Pascoe, Cambridge Spies, Lloyd And Hill, Band Of Brothers, Love In A Cold Climate, Aristocrats, Cider With Rosie, The Jump, The Unknown Soldier, Holding On, Cold Lazarus, Touch of Frost.* Film includes: *Scoop, Partition, Heights, Ascension, Lion In Winter, Benedict Arnold, The Good Pope, Dk2, Trance, Purpose, Investigating Sex, 5 Seconds To Spare, A Rather English Marriage, Mrs Pollifax, Keep It on the Lowdown.* Radio includes: *Man and Boy, Minuet, The Razor's Edge, Les Parents Terribles.*

Mark Meadows (*Spini* / Musical Director)
Theatre includes: *Macbeth, A Midsummer Night's Dream* (Open Air Theatre, Regent's Park); *White Christmas* (Theatre Royal, Plymouth/Mayflower, Southampton); *Mary Poppins* (Prince Edward Theatre); *Longitude* (Greenwich Theatre); *5/11, Lee Miller, King Lear* (Chichester Festival Theatre); *Wonderful Town* (Grange Park Opera); *The Emperor and the Nightingale* (Watermill, Newbury); *High Society* (Sheffield Crucible); *Up the Feeder, Aeroplane Bones, Look Back in Anger, A Streetcar Named Desire* (Bristol Old Vic); *Noel and Gertie* (Eye Theatre). Television: *Casualty.* Film includes: *Nicholas Nickleby, High Heels and Lowlifes.*

Richard Moore (*Old Vito*)
Theatre includes: *In the Club* (Hampstead Theatre); *The Winter's Tale, Pericles, Waiting for Godot, Under Milk Wood, Lynchville, Dumb Waiter, Merry Wives of Windsor, Two Gentlemen of Verona, Romeo and Juliet, Henry V, Richard II, Troilus and Cressida, Midsummer Night's Dream, Hamlet, As You Like It* (RSC); *Dead Funny, Ink and Urine, Merry Wives of Windsor, The Visit, The Silver King, Three Men in a Boat* (Chichester Festival Theatre); *Rosencrantz & Guildenstern are Dead, An Evening*

with *Charles Dickens* (Theatr Clwyd/tour); *King Lear* (Theatr Clwyd); *Two Clouds Over Eden* (Manchester Royal Exchange); *Twelfth Night, Hay Fever, Educating Rita, Passion Play, Hedda Gabler, School for Scandal, The Cherry Orchard, Much Ado About Nothing, Hamlet, Taming of the Shrew* (Leicester Haymarket); *Merry Wives of Windsor* (National Theatre); *Macbeth, The Connection, The Samaritan, Hans Kolhaas, The Tribades, Quantrille In Lawrence, The Passion Of Dracula* (London/West End); *The Birdwatchers, King Lear, As You Like It* (Australia). Television includes: *Gold Plated, Emmerdale, Born & Bred, Where The Heart Is, Heartbeat, The Mayor of Casterbridge, Nearest and Dearest, Band of Gold, Wycliffe, House of Elliot, Enemy at the Door, Boon, Good as Gold, Chancer, The Professionals, The Likely Lads, Z Cars.* Film includes: *Fanny and Elvis, The Human Bomb, Blue Juice, Deadly Advice, Robin Hood, Death of a Son, Lady Jane, Juggernaut, The Offence, The Raging Moon.*

Stephen Noonan (*Machiavelli*)
Theatre includes: *Faustus* (Hampstead Theatre); *The Odyssey* (Lyric Hammersmith); *Enemies* (Almeida); *King Lear, 5/11* (Chichester Festival Theatre); *Volpone* (Manchester Royal Exchange); *Hamlet* (Southampton); *Jubilee, Love in a Wood* (RSC); *Macbeth* (Stratford/Tokyo/New Haven); *Gross Indecency* (Gielgud); *The Misanthrope, Major Barbara* (Piccadilly); *Cloud Nine, The Provok'd Wife, King Lear, Playhouse Creatures, Wind in the Willows* (Old Vic); *Enjoy* (Nottingham Playhouse); *Hamlet* (Tour/West End). Television includes: *E=MC2, Waking the Dead, The Divine Michaelangelo, VIII, Ultimate Force, Death in Holy Orders, Small Potatoes, Comedy Nation, The Bill, Dangerfield, Peak Practice, London's Burning.* Film includes: *Clarion's Call, Blackball, I'll Be There, Gypsy Woman, Macbeth, The Affair of the Necklace, Cassandra's Dream.*

Simon Trinder (*Salai*)
Theatre includes: *Buried Alive* (Hampstead Theatre); *The Tempest* (Manchester Royal Exchange); *Merry Wives - The Musical, Pedro, The Great Pretender, House of Desires, The Dog in the Manger, Visible, The Taming of the Shrew, The Tamer Tamed, Measure For Measure, Cymbeline, Birdsong* (RSC); *A Midsummer Night's Dream* (Hamburg State Opera); *Tintin* (Barbican); *The Arab Israeli Cookbook* (Tricycle); *The Importance of Being Earnest* (Bristol Old Vic); *Peter Pan* (Birmingham Rep); *A Midsummer Night's Dream, The Golden Ass* (Shakespeare's Globe); *A Christmas Carol* (Chichester Festival Theatre); *Redundant* (Royal Court). Film: *Keep it on the Lowdown.* Television includes: *Dalziel & Pascoe, In Search of Shakespeare, Holby City.* Radio includes: over 50 plays as a member of the BBC Radio Repertory Company.

Philip Voss (*Lodovico | Soderini*)
Philip Voss is an Associate Actor of the RSC and among the roles he has played for that company are Prospero, Malvolio, Menenius in *Coriolanus,* Cardinal Monticelso in *The White Devil,* Sir Epicure Mammon in *The Alchemist,* Peter Quince in *A Midsummer Night's Dream* and Ulysses in *Troilus and Cressida.* He last worked with Gregory

Doran at the Royal Shakespeare Company playing Shylock in *The Merchant of Venice*. For the Royal National Theatre: Rodin in *The Wandering Jew*, Ferdinando in *Countrymania*, James in *The Strangeness of Others*, Juster in *Abingdon Square*, Count Shabelsky in *Ivanov*, Boyet in Sir Trevor Nunn's productions of *Love's Labour's Lost*, Miguel Estete in *The Royal Hunt of the Sun*. His other work in London includes: for Shared Experience – Doctor Dorn in *The Seagull*, Dr Chebutykin in *Three Sisters* and Kochkaryov in *Marriage* and most recently Jaques in Sir Peter Hall's productions of *As You Like It* both in England and America, *The Royal Family* and *Much Ado About Nothing*. He performed at the original Hampstead Theatre in *Short List* by Michael Rudman and *Particular Friendships* by Martyn Allen – directed respectively by Mike Ockrent and Michael Attenborough. Film includes: *Brides in the Bath*, *The Dwelling Place*, *Let Them Eat Cake*, *Octopussy*, *Four Weddings and a Funeral*, *Frankenstein and the Monster from Hell*, *Alive and Kicking*. Recent radio includes: Simon Gary's *Little Nell*.

Gregory Doran (Director)
Theatre includes for the RSC: Chief Associate Director. As Director: *The Odyssey*, *Henry VIII*, *Cyrano de Bergerac*, *The Merchant of Venice*, *The Winter's Tale*, *Oroonoko*, *Timon of Athens*, *Macbeth*, *As You Like It*, *King John*, *Jubilee*, *Much Ado About Nothing*, *The Island Princess*, Director of Jacobeans Season 2002 (Olivier Award for Outstanding Achievement of the Year 2003), *The Taming of the Shrew*, *The Tamer Tamed*, *All's Well That Ends Well*, *Othello*, *Venus and Adonis*, *A Midsummer Night's Dream*, *Sejanus: His Fall*, Director of Gunpowder Season 2005, *The Canterbury Tales*, *Antony and Cleopatra*, *The Rape of Lucrece*, *Merry Wives the Musical*, *Coriolanus*, *Venus and Adonis*. Other theatre includes: *The Real Inspector Hound/Black Comedy* (Donmar/West End); *Mahler's Conversion* (Aldwych); *Titus Andronicus* (Market Theatre Johannesburg/National Theatre Studio); *The Joker of Seville* (Boston/Trinidad); *Someone to Watch Over Me* (Theatr Clwyd); *The Importance of Being Earnest*, *Bedroom Farce*, *An Inspector Calls*, *Private Lives* (Century Theatre); *Long Day's Journey into Night*, *Waiting for Godot*, *The Norman Conquests* (Nottingham Playhouse).Television includes: Michael Wood's *In Search of Shakespeare*, *Midsummer Night's Dreaming*. Film includes: *Macbeth* (Illuminations/Channel 4). Writing: Co-author (with Antony Sher) of *Woza Shakespeare!*

William Dudley (Designer)
Theatre includes: *Some Sunny Day* (Hampstead Theatre); *Small Change*, *The Fool*, *Edmund*, *Hamlet*, *Etta Jenks*, *Kafka's Dick* (Royal Court); *I Licked A Slag's Deodorant* (Royal Court/Ambassadors); *Hitchcock Blonde* (Olivier Award - At Royal Court/South Coast Repertory Theatre, California); *Ivanov*, *That Good Between Us*, *Richard III*, *The Party*, *The Merry Wives of Windsor* (Olivier Award), *Richard II*, *A Midsummer Night's Dream*, *Country Dancing*, *The General from America*, *The Ship*, *The Big Picnic* (RSC); *Marya* (RSC/Old Vic); *Hamlet* (RSC/Neue Schauspielhaus Hamburg); *I Claudius*, *Mutiny!*, *Kiss Me Kate*, *Girlfriends*, *Matador*, *Heartbreak House*, *My Night With Reg*, *Rat in the Skull*, *A Streetcar*

Named Desire, Lenny, Entertaining Mr Sloane, Blue/Orange, The Breath Of Life (West End); The York Realist (West End/English Touring Theatre/Royal Court); Hitchcock Blonde (West End/Royal Court); The Woman In White (West End/Broadway); Lavender Blue, Larkrise To Candleford, Lost Worlds, The World Turned Upside Down, Undiscovered Country, Dispatches (Olivier Award), Don Quixote, Schweyk in the Second World War, The Real Inspector Hound, The Critic, The Mysteries (Olivier Award), Entertaining Strangers, Waiting for Godot, Cat on a Hot Tin Roof, The Shaughraun, The Changeling, Bartholomew Fair, The Voysey Inheritance, The Crucible, The Coup, Pygmalion, The Rise And Fall of Little Voice (Olivier Award), On The Ledge, Johnny on a Spot, Under Milk Wood, Wild Oats, Mary Stuart, The Homecoming, The London Cuckolds, Cleo Camping Emmanuelle and Dick, The Forest, Blue/Orange, All My Sons (Olivier Award 2001: Best Set Designer), The Coast Of Utopia, Honour, The Permanent Way, Cyrano De Bergerac, Landscape With Weapon, The Hothouse (National Theatre); The Alchemist (National Theatre/Birmingham Repertory Theatre); Old Times, Betrayal (Donmar Warehouse); The Deep Blue Sea, Tongue of a Bird (Almeida Theatre); Titus Andronicus (Globe Theatre); Look Back in Anger (Theatre Royal Bath); The Last Confession (Chichester Festival Theatre/West End). William also designed the sets for Roman Polanski's acclaimed musical version of The Dance Of The Vampires, which opened in Vienna in October 1997 then toured Germany, opening in Berlin in early 2007, and for Peter Hall's production of Amadeus at the Old Vic and Broadway. Opera includes: Idomeneo (WNO); Billy Budd (Metropolitan Opera); Barber of Seville, Seraglio (Glyndebourne); Tales Of Hoffman, Der Rosenkavalier, Don Giovanni, The Cunning Little Vixen (ROH); The Ring Cycle (Bayreuth); Un Ballo in Maschera (Salzburg Festival); Lucia Di Lammermoor (Lyric Opera of Chicago); Lucia Di Lammermoor (Opera National de Paris); The Silver Tassie (ENO). Film includes: Persuasion (BAFTA Winner), The Rose Theatre (Royal Television Society Winner). William has won seven Olivier Awards and been nominated for a further seven. He received a BAFTA and a Royal Television Society Award for his work on Persuasion (BBC). He was nominated for two Outer Critics Circle awards for scenic and costume design for Amadeus on Broadway. Bill won the 2003 Critics Circle Award for The Coast of Utopia (National Theatre) and was nominated for both the Evening Standard Award and the Olivier Award for the same production. He won the Theatregoers' Choice Award for Best Set Designer for The Woman in White in 2005.

Oliver Fenwick (Lighting Designer)
Theatre credits include: Glass Eels, Comfort Me with Apples (Hampstead Theatre); She Stoops To Conquer (Birmingham Rep); Kean (Apollo Theatre, West End); Pure Gold (Soho Theatre); Henry V, Mirandolina (Royal Exchange); Restoration (Bristol Old Vic/tour for Headlong); My Fair Lady (Cameron Mackintosh/National Theatre Tour production); The Caretaker, Comedy of Errors, Bird Calls, Iphigenia (Crucible Theatre, Sheffield); A Doll's House (West Yorkshire Playhouse); Sunshine on Leith

(Dundee Rep & Tour); *Heartbreak House* (Watford Palace); *A Model Girl* (Greenwich Theatre); *The Solid Gold Cadillac* (Garrick Theatre, West End); *The Secret Rapture* (Lyric Shaftesbury Avenue); *Noises Off, All My Sons, Dr Faustus* (Liverpool Playhouse); *On the Piste* (Birmingham Rep); *The Chairs* (Gate Theatre); *Follies, Insignificance, Breaking the Code* (Theatre Royal, Northampton); *Tartuffe, The Gentleman from Olmedo, The Venetian Twins, Hobson's Choice, Dancing at Lughnasa, Love in a Maze* (Watermill Theatre); *Fields of Gold, Villette* (Stephen Joseph Theatre); *Cinderella* (Bristol Old Vic); *Hysteria, Children of a Lesser God* (Salisbury Playhouse). Opera credits include: *Samson et Delilah, Lohengrin* (Royal Opera House); *The Trojan Trilogy* and *The Nose* (Linbury ROH); *The Gentle Giant* (The Clore ROH); *The Threepenny Opera* (for the Opera Group); *L'Opera Seria* (Batignano Festival).

Matt McKenzie (Sound Designer)
Theatre includes as a Sound Designer: *Favourite Nights, Rents, Brittanicus, Noises Off, The White Glove, The Provok'd Wife, Private Dick, Miss Julie, Hobson's Choice, Mass Appeal, Crime and Punishment, Lent and The Man Who Fell in Love with His Wife, Angry Housewives, The Hypochondriac, Faith Hope and Charity, Sailor Beware, Loot, Lady Audley's Secret, Madras House, The Way of the World, Ghost Train, Greasepaint, In the Summer House, Exact Change* (Lyric Hammersmith); *Macbeth* (Nuffield Theatre Southampton); *Una Pooka* (Tricyle); *Vertigo, That Good Night, Hinge of the World* (Guildford); *Saturday Sunday Monday, Easy Virtue, The Seagull, A Midsummer Night's Dream, Master and Margarita, 5/11, Nicholas Nickleby* (Chichester Festival Theatre); *Dracula, Frankenstein, A Midsummer Night's Dream, Macbeth* (Derby Playhouse); *Flamingos, Damages, After The End* (Bush Theatre); *Made in Bangkok, The House of Bernarda Alba, A Piece of My Mind, Journey's End, A Madhouse in Goa, Barnaby and the Old Boys, Irma Vep, Gasping, Map of the Heart, Tango Argentino, When She Danced, Misery, Murder is Easy, The Odd Couple, Pygmalion, Things We Do for Love, Long Day's Journey Into Night, Macbeth, Sexual Perversity in Chicago, Calico, A Life in the Theatre, Swimming With Sharks* (West End); *Lysistrata, The Master Builder, School for Wives, Mind Millie for Me, A Streetcar Named Desire, Three of a Kind* (Sir Peter Hall); *Amadeus* (Sir Peter Hall/West End/Broadway); *Leaves of Glass, Baghdad Wedding* (Soho Theatre); *Frame312, After Miss Julie, Days of Wine and Roses* (Donmar); *Iron and The People Next Door* (The Traverse). He was Sound Supervisor for the Peter Hall Seasons at The Old Vic and The Piccadilly and designed the sound for *Waste, Cloud 9, The Seagull, The Provok'd Wife, King Lear, The Misanthrope, Major Barbara, Filumena, Kafka's Dick. Family Reunion, Henry V, The Duchess of Mafli, Hamlet, The Lieutenant of Inishmore, Julius Caesar* and *A Midsummer Night's Dream* (RSC). Matt's musical work includes: *Love off the Shelf* (Nuffield Theatre); *The Bells are Ringing, Talk of the Steamie* (Greenwich); *Forbidden Broadway, Blues in the Night* (West End); Matthew Bourne's *Car Man* (West End/International Tour); *Putting it Together, The Gondoliers, How to*

Succeed in Business Without Really Trying, Carousel, Babes In Arms (Chichester); Oh! What A Lovely War, A Christmas Carol, Sweeney Todd, Company, Into the Woods, Merrily We Roll Along, Moon Landing (Derby Playhouse); Mark Ravenhill's Dick Whittington (Barbican).

Paul Englishby (Composer)

Theatre includes: Yellowman, Anna in the Tropics (Hampstead Theatre); Coriolanus, Merry Wives the Musical, A Midsummer Night's Dream, Sejanus, Much Ado About Nothing, The Merchant of Venice, The Taming of the Shrew, The Tamer Tamed, All's Well That Ends Well (RSC); Sugar Mummies, Blood (Royal Court); Longitude (Greenwich); Three Sisters, Romeo and Juliet (Chichester); Visitation (Oval House); Amnesia (Young Vic); Bedroom Farce (West End). Television as Composer: The Score, History of Football, Pictures on the Piano, Human Jungle, Hidden Voices, Living with the Enemy. Film includes as Composer: Miss Pettigrew Lives for a Day (Forthcoming), Magicians, Confetti, Ten Minutes Older – The Trumpet, Ten Minutes Older – The Cello, The Enlightenment, Serial Thriller, Death of the Revolution. As a Arranger/Orchestrator: Becoming Jane, Goal 2, Proof, Captain Corelli's Mandolin, Animal, The Altzheimer Case, Proof, Two Brothers, Birthday Girl, Hart's War, Charlotte Gray, Secret Passage, If Only, Love's Brother. As Musical Director: Alpha Male, The Feast of the Goat, If Only, About a Boy, Hart's War, Captain Corelli's Mandolin, Flawless, Miguel and William, Deseo, Love's Brother, Black Ball. Concert Hall credits include: Music in Motion, Byron, Violin Concerto, Short Symphony, Sonata for String Quartet, Dots for wind quintet, Lyrics for violin and cello, Don't Try This at Home for solo piano, Lullaby for flute and piano, The Child Ephemeral for organ, Sonnet VIII for tenor voice and string quartet, I am Music for school choirs and orchestra, Weep no More for strings, Everything is You for saxophone quartet.

Mel Cook (Assistant Director)

Mel trained at RADA. Theatre includes as Assistant Director: Life After Scandal (Hampstead Theatre). As Director: A Midsummer Night's Dream (Jesus College); A Christmas Carol (Southwark Playhouse); Telltales (Theatre 503) and several Start Night and youth productions, for Hampstead Theatre, the Arcola, Stratford and the New Wimbledon. She has been long and shortlisted for the JMK, C4, and OSBTTA young director's awards. As actor: Carver (Arcola); Taming of the Shrew (UK tour); Macbeth (UK tour); Boudicca (Eastern Angles); Les Liasons Dangereuses (RADA); Love's Labour's Lost (Drill Hall); Tempest (Graeae). As an improviser, Mel has developed and toured shows from Chicago to Auckland via Glastonbury, ITV and Channel 4. She is currently devising work for Shakespeare's Globe.

hampsteadtheatre

hampsteadtheatre is one of the UK's leading new-writing venues housed in a magnificent purpose-built state-of-the-art theatre – a company that is fast approaching its fiftieth year of operation.

hampsteadtheatre has a mission: to find, develop, and produce new plays to the highest possible standards, for as many people as we can encourage to see them. Its work is both national and international in its scope and ambition.

hampsteadtheatre exists to take risks and to discover the talent of the future. New writing is our passion. We consistently create the best conditions for writers to flourish and are rewarded with diverse award-winning and far-reaching plays.

The list of playwrights who had their early work produced at **hampstead**theatre who are now filling theatres all over the country and beyond include Mike Leigh, Michael Frayn, Brian Friel, Terry Johnson, Hanif Kureishi, Simon Block, Abi Morgan, Rona Munro, Tamsin Oglesby, Harold Pinter, Philip Ridley, Shelagh Stephenson, debbie tucker green, Crispin Whittell and Roy Williams. The careers of actors Jude Law, Alison Steadman, Jane Horrocks and Rufus Sewell were launched at **hampstead**theatre.

Each year the theatre invites the most exciting writers around to write for us. At least half of these playwrights will be emerging writers who are just hitting their stride – writers who we believe are on the brink of establishing themselves as important new voices. We also ask mid-career and mature playwrights to write for us on topics they are burning to explore.

the success of **hampstead**theatre is yours to support

hampsteadtheatre exists to present new writing for the stage. After years of outstanding work, the theatre now has a home to match its reputation – a home which will continue to produce some of the most exhilarating theatre in London.

In order to continue to develop and produce new plays to an international standard, as well as extending our Creative Learning programmes to local schools and community groups, providing the opportunity for people to improve their literacy and creative skills, we need your help.

By becoming one of our Luminaries, you will be giving vital support to all aspects of the theatre's work. There are six levels that provide fantastic benefits, allowing you to get the most out of your visit to the theatre.

Level One – £100 per year

- Early discount offer and priority booking for all our productions
- Dedicated booking line to the Box Office Manager
- Advance information about productions and events
- Crediting as a supporter in our production programmes and on our website
- An invitation to a Question-and-Answer Session with the Artistic Director

Level Two – £250 per year

As Level One with the additional benefits of:

- One pair of complimentary tickets to five productions throughout the year
- Invitation to special theatre events
- Private backstage tour, by arrangement

Level Three – £1,000 per year

As Level Two with the additional benefits of:

- Complimentary interval drinks with each pair of tickets
- An opportunity to attend private readings of plays in development
- Priority booking for press night and access to a special drinks area on press nights
- 20% discount on food and drinks at our Café Bar
- Private bookings through the Development Department
- Opportunity to book house seats when a production is officially 'Sold Out' (subject to availability)

Level Four – £2,500 per year

As Level Three with the additional benefits of:

- Annual production support by Level Four Luminaries
- Exclusive event associated with the supported production
- An invitation to opening night when a production is transferred to the West End

Level Five - £5,000 per year

As Level Four with the additional benefits of:

- Four complimentary tickets to five productions throughout the year
- A special Supper Club evening with the cast
- Annual Lunch with the Artistic Director

Production Syndicate – £10,000 per year

As Level Five with the additional benefits of:

- Highest priority for all bookings including short-notice requests
- Opportunity to host a private theatre party for twenty people, with exclusive use of boardroom for pre- or post-performance receptions (catering not included)

our current luminaries are:

(as of October 2008)

Production Syndicate
Lloyd & Sarah Dorfman

Level 5
Elizabeth & Daniel Peltz
Mr & Mrs E McGregor

Level 4
Leonard Eppel CBE &
  Barbara Eppel
Sir Richard Eyre
Sir Clement & Lady Jill Freud
Arnold Fulton
Midge & Simon Palley
Richard Peskin
Wendy & Peter Phillips
Paul Rayden
Anthony Simmonds
The Peter Wolff Theatre
  Trust

Level 3
Pauline & Daniel Auerbach
Dorothy & John Brook
The Sidney & Elizabeth
  Corob Foundation
David Cohen
Professor & Mrs C J
  Dickinson
David Dutton
George & Rosamund
  Fokschaner
Michael Frayn
Jacqueline & Michael Gee
Jay Harris
Rachele & John Harrison
Michael & Morven Heller
J Leon & Company Ltd
David & Wendy Meller
Brian & Hilary Pomeroy
Michael & Livia Prior
Paul & Claire Rayden
Sue & Anthony Rosner
Sir David Scholey
Judy Williams

Level 2
Jenny Abramsky CBE
Bob Ainscow
Anonymous
Lesley Bennett
The Ben-Levi Family
Judith & Shmuel Ben-Tovim

Karen Brown & John Blake
Bob & Jenni Buhr
Geraldine Caulfield
Jessica & Shimon Cohen
Robyn Durie
Bernard Faber
Frankie de Freitas
Susan & Jeremy Freeman
Jacqueline & Jonathan
  Gestetner
Richard Gladstone
Anthony Goldstein
Conway Van Gelder Grant
  Ltd
P & F Hackworth
Elaine & Peter Hallgarten
Robin & Inge Hyman
Paul Jenkins
Harold Joels
Norman & Doreen Joels
Patricia Karet
Tony Klug & Joanne
  Edelman
David Lanch
Alasdair Liddell
Brian & Anne Lapping
Paul & Paula Marber
Julia & Julian Markson
Myra & Alec Marmot
Tom & Karen Mautner
Judith Mishon
Sandy & David Montague
Edna & Jerrold Moser
Nicholas Murphy
Trevor Phillips
Clare Rich
Rita & Anthony Rose
The Rubin Foundation
Marcus & Andrea Sarner
Isabelle & Ivor Seddon
James Barrington Serjent
Dr Michael Spiro
Revd Derek & Mrs Estelle
  Spottiswoode
Jonathan Stone
Clive Swift
Talbot Designs
Christopher Wade
Tom Wedgwood
Hugh Whitemore & Rohan
  McCullouch
Adrian Whiteson
Denise Winton

Della Worms & Fred Worms
  OBE
Stanley Wright

Level 1
Anonymous
David Adams
Lord Archer
Regina Aukin
Graham & Michelle Barber
Eric & Jean Beecham
Arline Blass
Alan Brodie Representation
Leonard Bull
Deborah Buzan
Suzy Korel Casting
June Cowan
Mr & Mrs Michael David
Jose & David Dent
Ralph Emanuel
Peter English
Eva & Desmond Feldman
Richard Foster
Bobbie Ginswick
Mitchell Gitin
Desmond Goch
G C Goldman
Linda Goldman
Paul Harris
Simon Jones
Anna Katz
Lady Keegan
Siegi & Valerie Mandelbaum
David & Sandra Max
Raymond Mellor
Roger & Bridget Myddelton
Thomas Neumark
Rafe & Stacey Offer
Tamara & Michael Rabin
Claudia Rosoux
Peter Roth QC
Lady Solti
Bonnie Tabatznik
Ann Vernau
Tim Watson
Cecilia Wong
Anna C Young
Derek Zissman

thank you to the following for supporting our creativity:

Abbey Charitable Trust; Acacia Charitable Trust; Anglo American; Arimathea Charitable Trust; Arts & Business; Awards for All; The Alchemy Foundation; Auerbach Trust Charity; Bank Leumi; BBC Children in Need; Bennetts Associates; Big Lottery Fund; Blick Rothenberg; Bridge House Estates Trust Fund; Swiss Cottage Area Partnership; Community Fund; The John S Cohen Foundation; Coutts Charitable Trust; D'Oyly Carte Charitable Trust; The Dorset Foundation; Duis Charitable Trust; The Eranda Foundation; The Ernest Cook Trust; European Association of Jewish Culture; Garrick Charitable Trust; Gerald Ronson Foundation; The Goldsmiths Company; The Hampstead & Highgate Express; Hampstead, Wells & Campden Trust; Help a London Child; Harold Hyam Wingate Foundation; The Jack Petchey Foundation; Jacobs Charitable Trust; John Lyon's Charitable Trust; Lloyds TSB Foundation for England and Wales; Kennedy Leigh Charitable Trust; Local Network Fund; Mackintosh Foundation; Markson Pianos; Marriot Hotel, Regents Park; Milly Apthorp Charitable Trust; The Mirianog Trust; The Morel Trust: The Noël Coward Foundation; Notes Productions Ltd; Ocado; The Ormonde & Mildred Duveen Trust; Parkheath Estates: The Paul Hamlyn Foundation: The Rayne Foundation; Reed Elsevier; Richard Grand Foundation; Richard Reeves Foundation; Royal Victoria Hall Foundation; Samuel French; The Shoresh Foundation; Sir John Cass' Foundation; Society for Theatre Research; Solomon Taylor Shaw: Sweet and Maxwell; Karl Sydow; Towry Law; The Vintners' Company; World Jewish Relief; Charles Wolfson Foundation.

If you would like to become more closely involved, and would like to help us find the talent and the audiences of the future, please call Tamzin Robertson on 020 7449 4171 or email development@hampsteadtheatre.com.

capital campaign supporters

hampsteadtheatre would like to thank the following donors who kindly contributed to the Capital Campaign, enabling us to build our fantastic new home.

Mr Robert Adams
Mr Robert Ainscow
Mrs Farah Alaghband
Mr W Aldwinckle
Mr Mark Allison
Anonymous
Mrs Klari Atkin
Mr William Atkins
Mr and Mrs Daniel and Pauline Auerbach
Mr David Aukin
Sir Alan Ayckbourn
Mr George Bailey
Mr Christopher Beard
Mr Eric Beecham
Mrs Lucy Ben-Levi
Mr Alan Bennett
Mr and Mrs Rab Bennetts
Mr Roger Berlind
Ms Vicky Biles
Mr Michael Blakemore
Mr Simon Block
Mr A Bloomfield
Mr John Bolton
Mr Peter Borender
Mr and Mrs Rob and Colleen Brand
Mr Matthew Broadbent
Mr Alan Brodie
Dr John and Dorothy Brook
Mr Leonard Bull
Mr and Mrs Paul and Ossie Burger
Ms Kathy Burke
Mr O Burstin
Ms Deborah Buzan
Mr Charles Caplin
Sir Trevor and Susan Chinn
Mr Martin Cliff
Mr Michael Codron
Mr and Mrs Denis Cohen
Dr David Cohen
Mr David Cornwell
Mr and Mrs Sidney and Elizabeth Corob
Mr and Mrs John Crosfield
Miss Nicci Crowther
Ms Hilary Dane
Mr and Mrs Ralph Davidson
Mr and Mrs Gerald Davidson
Mrs Deborah Davis
Mr Edwin Davison
Mr David Day
Ms Frankie de Freitas
Mr and Mrs David and Jose Dent

Professor Christopher and Elizabeth Dickinson
Sir Harry Djanogly
Ms Lindsay Duncan
Mr David Dutton
Mrs Myrtle Ellenbogen
Mr Michael Elwyn
Mr Tom Erhardt
Sir Richard Eyre
Mr Peter Falk
Ms Nina Finburgh
Mr and Mrs George and Rosamund Fokschaner
Ms Lisa Forrell
Mr N Forsyth
Mr Freddie Fox
Mr Michael Frayn
Mr Norman Freed
Mr Conrad Freedman
Mr and Mrs Robert and Elizabeth Freeman
Mr and Mrs Jeremy and Susan Freeman
Mr and Mrs Brian Friel
Mr Arnold Fulton
Mr and Mrs Michael and Jacqueline Gee
Mr and Mrs Jonathan and Jacqueline Gestetner
Mr Desmond Goch
Mr Anthony Goldstein
Mr Andrew Goodman
Ms Niki Gorick
Mrs Katerina Gould
Lord and Lady Grabiner
Mr and Mrs Jonathan Green
Mr and Mrs David Green
Mrs Susan Green
Mr Nicholas Greenstone
Mr Michael Gross
Mr and Mrs Paul Hackworth
Dr Peter and Elaine Hallgarten
Miss Susan Hampshire
Mr Christopher Hampton
Mr Laurence Harbottle
Sir David Hare
Lady Pamela Harlech
Mr Paul Harris
Mr John Harrison
Mr Howard Harrison
Mr Jonathan Harvey
Sir Maurice Hatter
Mr Marc Hauer
Dr Samuel Hauer
Mr and Mrs Michael and Morven Heller

Mr Philip Hobbs
Mr and Mrs Robin and Inge Hyman
Mr Nicholas Hytner
Ms Phoebe Isaacs
Mr Michael Israel
Professor Howard and Sandra Jacobs
Mr and Mrs Max Jacobs
Dr C Kaplanis
Mrs Patricia Karet
Baroness Helena Kennedy
Mrs Ann Kieran
Mr Jeremy King
Mr Peter Knight
Sir Eddie Kulukundis
Ms Belinda Lang
Mr and Mrs Edward Lee
Mrs Janette Lesser
Lady Diane Lever
Mr Daniel Levy
Mr Peter Levy
Sir Sydney and Lady Lipworth
Mrs Alyssa Lovegrove
Ms Sue MacGregor
Mr S Magee
Mr Fouad Malouf
Mr and Mrs Lee Manning
Mr and Mrs Thomas and Karen Mautner
Mr and Mrs David and Sandra Max
Mrs June McCall
Mr John McFadden
Mr Ewan McGregor
Mr and Mrs David Meller
Mr Raymond Mellor
Mr Anthony Minghella
Mr and Mrs David Mirvish
Mr and Mrs Mark Mishon
Mr and Mrs Edward and Diana Mocatta
Mr and Mrs Gary Monnickendam
Mrs and Mrs David and Sandra Montague
Mr Peter Morris
Mr and Mrs Ian Morrison
Mr Andrew Morton
Lady Sara Morton
Mr Gabriel Moss QC
Mr and Mrs Terence Mugliston
Mr and Mrs Roger and Bridget Myddelton
Mr Stewart Nash
Mr James Nederlander

hampsteadtheatre would also like to thank the many generous donors who we are unable to list individually.

creative learning
widening access to new playwriting

Changing Lives

Our Creative Learning programme is a thriving part of **hampstead**theatre's work. We aim to celebrate all aspects of the creative process in ways which support learning and widen access to the theatre's programme. At its best, our work has the power to change lives.

'My first encounter with Hampstead Theatre was a primary school trip when I was 8 years old. I am now a Peer Ambassador, which involves teaching and assisting drama projects for a range of different age groups. The experience has really boosted my confidence and has made me value responsibility.'
(Youth Theatre Member since 2003)

We work closely with **hampstead**theatre artists and writers to find innovative ways to inspire creativity and develop emerging talent. The programme helps people of all ages to develop personal, social and communication skills. We actively engage with some of the most disadvantaged groups in our local community.

Schools Audiences – Follow Spot

We're offering a limited number of £6 tickets for Excellence In Cities schools in Greater London (available to groups attending midweek matinees and designated performances only). All other schools tickets are £10, with one free ticket for every ten paid.

Our schools audience programme makes a visit to see a show at **hampstead**theatre more meaningful, accessible and educational. Follow Spot offers exciting creative strategies for delivering the curriculum, exploring the creative practice behind a production, and increasing understanding of the creative industries. We provide:

- Free online teacher resources, including complete schemes of work for GCSE and A-Level
- Free play texts (when making a booking)
- Free post-show Q&A with the company and creative team
- Teacher trainings with director or writer (subject to availability, £5 per teacher)
- Bespoke pre- or post-visit workshops

'An inspiration!' 'A real refreshment of skills and ideas.'
'Excellent techniques that I can translate into my own work.'
(Teachers attending training in June 2007)

Call our Schools Tickets Co-ordinator on 020 7722 9301 to book.

Boosting Learning

At the heart of the programme is a network of long-term relationships with teachers and young people at local schools. Through in-school workshops, theatre visits and youth theatre referrals, we help to improve learning, motivation and self esteem. Our script and story-writing projects, for example, offer new, drama-based ways to improve literacy, which in turn boosts learning across all subjects in the curriculum.

'The programme that our school has created in collaboration with Hampstead Theatre and the Royal Court is extensive and is absolutely key to the success of the department, both in terms of exam results and also the wider and less easily evaluated development of students creativity and self worth.'
(Head Of Drama, local secondary school, March 2007)

Act, Write and More with Our Youth Theatre

The **heat**&**light** Company is made up of budding performers, writers, directors, stage managers and technicians aged 11 to 25. Each term four groups come together to explore the power and potential of theatre in ways which reflect the artistic practice at Hampstead. This year our groups have worked with nine writers, including John Donnelly, Nick Grosso and Steve Waters, as well as John Kani and the *Nothing But The Truth* company. **hampstead**theatre's Youth Theatre is free to all participants and produces twelve performances a year.

'The first heat&light term was really good because it felt like there were no rules and you could write, act or do anything you wanted, with the freedom to perform and produce fresh and new ideas. The Daring Pairings project in which I co-wrote and produced a short play with Roy Williams was particularly enjoyable. I am now writing and acting for Channel 4's new show Skins.'
(Youth Theatre Member since 2003)

Creative Learning by Numbers

In the year April 06 – March 07 our outcomes included:

- 11,000 participants, of which 58% from a BME background, at 595 events
- 75 complete projects delivered at the theatre and out in school and community settings
- 83 educational performances in the Michael Frayn Space

If you would like to find out more please email
creativelearning@hampsteadtheatre.com

for **hampstead**theatre

Directors
Jenny Abramsky CBE (Chair)
David Adams FCA
Larry Billett
Paul Jenkins
Amanda Jones
Daniel Peltz
Michael Pennington
Paul Rayden
Greg Ripley-Duggan
Jeremy Sandelson

Company Secretary
Christopher Beard FCA

Advisory Council
Sir Trevor Chinn CVO
Michael Codron CBE
Lindsay Duncan
Michael Frayn
Sir Eddie Kulukundis OBE
Peter Phillips OBE
Patricia Rothman

Artistic Director
Anthony Clark

Executive Director
Bryan Savery

Literary
Associate Director (Literary) Frances Poet
Literary & Creative Learning Assistant
   Katy Silverton

Pearson Writer in Residence
   Alexis Zegerman
Channel 4 Theatre Director Scheme
   Noah Birksted-Breen

Administration
General Manager Neil Morris
Financial Controller Christopher Beard
Finance Officer Adam Halliday
Assistant to the Directorate Davina Shah
ITC Fast Track Trainee Brian Walters

Creative Learning
Creative Learning Director Eric Dupin
Schools Practitioner Debra Glazer
Literary & Creative Learning Assistant
   Katy Silverton

Marketing
Marketing Officer Vicky Brown
Press Officer Becky Sayer
Marketing Consultants
   makesthree Marketing & Promotion
   (anyone@makesthree.org)

Development
Development Director Sarah Coop
Development Manager Tamzin Robertson
Development Assistant Jon Opie
Events Manager Lady Lucy French

Production
Production Manager Tom Albu
Chief Electrician Kim O'Donoghue
Deputy Chief Electrician Sherry Coenen
Technical Manager David Tuff
Deputy Technical Manager
   Jonathan Goldstone
Technician (Michael Frayn Space)
   Cressida Klaces
Production Placement Shayna Petit

Box Office
Box Office Manager Chris Todd
Deputy Box Office Manager
   Caitriona Donaldson
Box Office Casuals
   Holly Mills, Kate Hewitt, Colin Knight,
   Lois Tucker, Maria Ferran, Oliver Meek,
   Paula Gray, Helen Matthews, Seamus
   Hewison, Steven Atkinson, Clare Betney,
   Lee Maxwell Simpson

Front of House
Front of House & Bar Manager David Scarr
Deputy Front of House Manager
   Virginia Aparicio
Duty Managers
   Jo Deakin, Robyn Wilson, Joanne Wilde,
   Sian Thomas
FOH Staff
   Alex Jenkinson, Alistair Murden, Amekia
   Cavollo, Asha Ramaswamy, Ben Groener,
   Daniel Kent, Florencia Cordeu, Geraldine
   Caulfield, Gwenllian Ash, Holly Reiss,
   Isaac Jones, Katy Bateman, Lindsey
   Crow, Max Davis, Sam Bailey, Rose
   Lewenstein, Sarah Page, Shane Craig,
   Tracey Button, Will Church, Lee Maxwell
   Simpson
Head Cleaner Rachael Marks
Cleaners Charmaine Ashman,
   Amina-O-Owusu

For Thelma Holt
Executive Director Malcolm Taylor
Assistant to Thelma Holt Anne Hudson
Production Manager Nick Ferguson
Head of Voice Margo Annett
Company Doctor Val Dias
Production Accountant Jim McCaul
Auditor Gorrie Whitson
Press Representative Peter Thompson
   Associates (020 7439 1210)
Marketing, Advertising & Graphics
   Dewynters (020 7321 0488)

WILL YOU?

Have you ever thought you could support
hampsteadtheatre by leaving a legacy?

hampsteadtheatre is a registered charity that exists
to present new writing for the stage. After years of
outstanding work, the theatre now has a home
to match its reputation for producing some of the most
exhilarating theatre in London.

In addition to producing ten full-scale productions
a year, we:

- Encourage diverse audiences to have a deeper
  understanding and appreciation of new plays in the
  theatre
- Support a successful integrated education
  programme that gives people, and young people in
  particular, the opportunity to participate in a wide
  range of writing and performance projects
- Read and respond to 1800 unsolicited scripts a year

hampsteadtheatre plays and will continue to play a
crucial role in the cultural life of its community.

If you leave a legacy to **hampstead**theatre this is free from tax.

For more information on leaving a legacy to
hampsteadtheatre, please get in touch with the Sarah Coop on
020 7449 4161 or email **sarahc@hampsteadtheatre.com**

Wine & dine for £25.00
in the Mediterrano Restaurant

Here's a really tasty offer. Enjoy a 3 course evening meal and a glass of house wine for just £25.00 in the Mediterrano Restaurant. How could you resist?

*For Richard Sharples, artist,
who first encouraged this play*

THE GIANT

Antony Sher

4

Author's Note

*'Some of Michelangelo's friends wrote from Florence to tell him
to return, since it was not beyond the realm of possibility that he
might be given the block of spoiled marble in the Works Department, which Piero Soderini, recently elected Gonfaloniere of the
city for life, had many times talked about giving to Leonardo da
Vinci . . . '*

This sentence in Giorgio Vasari's classic *The Lives of the Artists*
provided one of the sparks for writing *The Giant*, which is about
the carving of the statue of David. Another came from the book
David by the Hand of Michelangelo by the Renaissance scholar
Frederick Hartt, in which he suggests that a young mountaineer
quarryman from Carrara might have been the model for the
statue, because their daily labour produced a certain physical
build which corresponds to that of David.

Both Vasari and Hartt are giving voice to historical speculation
rather than historical fact – although a few of these exist too.
When, as an actor, I've played classical roles, I've always
enjoyed the way those playwrights, whether Shakespeare,
Marlowe or Massinger, regarded history simply as a springboard
for drama, using some bits, ditching others, inventing the rest.
Long before the term was invented, they knew that biopic was a
dull form. A plot started to cook in my head, mixing various
ingredients together: a fair amount of rumours and records from
the past along with a good helping of dramatic licence. The
starting point is certainly true: two giants of the Renaissance,
Leonardo and Michelangelo, were in the same city at the same
time. Nowadays it's generally accepted that both were gay – and
the city in question, Florence, was famously gay – yet they
seemed to have remained celibate. Why? I became more and
more drawn to exploring something which fascinates me: the link
between creativity and sexuality. And their link to power – for
Machiavelli was in Florence too.

When I was a schoolboy, and planning to go to art rather than drama school, my favourite artist was Michelangelo (at the time I wouldn't have been able to admit this was partly because of his obsession with the male nude), but during my early preparations for this play, Leonardo quickly became an equally if not more compelling figure for me. While Michelangelo creates giants – not just the statue of David, not just the Sistine Chapel, but the dome of St Peter's itself! – Leonardo works on a smaller scale. The Mona Lisa is not a big painting, and his codices (notebooks) are miniatures, yet contain some of his greatest achievements, as he tries to imagine and design things – such as aeroplanes – which will transform human life, even if the machinery of his time isn't yet capable of building them. I love Freud's description of Leonardo as a man waking too early in the dark while everyone else is still asleep.

I showed an outline of the play to the RSC, and they commissioned me to write it. Now my research intensified, although still just from books – books of words and books of pictures – and these yielded many surprises. I didn't know that Leonardo sat on the committee which decided where Michelangelo's David was to be placed. I didn't know that Leonardo became friends with Machiavelli while both were in attendance to Cesare Borgia. I didn't know that there's a sketch by Leonardo of Michelangelo's David. Or that, most startlingly, there's a portrait sketch by Michelangelo which is thought to be of Leonardo. (History records them meeting only once in a Florence street – a brief spat about Dante.) But I did know about their sketches for the 'Battle' frescoes which they were commissioned to paint side by side in the Signoria, and which neither accomplished. Both artists were notorious for not finishing commissions, but just imagine if they had finished that one.

My stack of books grew higher. If I was going to play around with history, I needed to know something about it first. The play is set at the beginning of the sixteenth century, when Florence was emerging from turbulent times. After the exile of their ruling family, the Medicis (following the death of Lorenzo the Magnificent in 1492), the city endured a period of extreme repression, Savonarola's rule. The fanatical friar recruited a Boy's Army, a sort of Hitler Youth, to intimidate the population, and to strip their homes of items as varied as mirrors, wigs, musical instruments and books for his Bonfires of the Vanities. Then Savonarola himself fell foul of the Vatican and was burnt at the stake in 1498. Florence had also survived the French invasion of Northern Italy, which left many of its neighbours, like Milan and Pisa, struggling to identify themselves politically. Meanwhile, Florence, now a free republic with a stable government, remained full of contra-dictions. It was known across Europe as a place of extreme licen-tiousness: it was, in a way, fulfilling Savonarola's direst prophecies, which warned that the city would become 'the Second Sodoma'. (The word sodomy referred to any unnatural sex acts in the Catholic sense – ie. not leading to procreation – whether between people of the same or opposite sex.) Yet at the same time, Florence still employed its formidable vice squad, the Officers of the Night, and if reported to them you could be in serious trouble.

But books are books. You can't smell Florence's river in a book, can't hear its pulse of insects, can't see the way its midsummer heat turns the terracotta roofs to a hazy white – you have to go there. And to the marble quarries at Carrara, which at a distance look like snowy alps, until you get close and realise that half the mountain is missing and you're seeing into its heart. And to Vinci, Leonardo's birthplace, which sits high on a Tuscan hilltop, and where you start to understand why he dreamed of flying.

These journeys, along with private views of Michelangelo's mighty David in its Florentine gallery and the beautiful ghost of Leonardo's ruined *The Last Supper* in its Milanese convent, as well as meetings with Italian scholars of Renaissance art and society – all these were made possible through the RSC's connec-tions to a certain Florentine mansion, the Villa La Pietra, once the home of the aesthete Sir Harold Acton, and subsequently bequeathed to New York University. Again and again, between 2005 and 2007, I travelled back and forth to Italy with my partner Greg Doran (the director of *The Giant*), and each time the Villa provided our contacts and our accommodation. Its long cyprus avenue with its curiously sloping dip, almost like a rope-bridge, the limonaia with its tall grey-green wooden doors, the terraced lawns and gardens which seem to hang above the city – these locations are lodged in my mind, and are an inseparable part of my preparations for *The Giant*. To someone whose previous projects have entailed meetings with murderers and journeys to Auschwitz, these new research trips were considerably more relaxing. There were times when I felt I was enjoying myself too much. But Greg always knew how to bring me back to earth. He'd say, 'Now all you have to do is write the play.'

I'm hugely indebted to Ellyn Toscano and Nick Dakin-Elliot at the Villa La Pietra, and to New York University. I also want to thank Hampstead Theatre, the RSC, and the producer Thelma Holt, for working together to make this production happen.

Antony Sher
London, September 2007

Acknowledgements

The author wishes to thank: Pietro Marani, Leonardo scholar at the Art Library, Castello Sforzesco, Milan; Bruce Edelstein, Michelangelo scholar, Florence; Giandomenico Semeraro, art scholar, Florence; Giovanni Cipriani, Renaissance historian, Florence; Ludovica Sebregondi, Savonarola scholar, Florence; Patrizia Asproni, Cultural Director of Giunti Publishers, Florence; Magda Nabb, author, Florence; Franco Barattini, owner of the Michelangelo Quarry, Carrara; Luciano Massari, sculptor at the Art Studio of the Michelangelo Quarry, Carrara; Hugo Chapman, curator of Italian drawings before 1800, British Museum, London; Rowan Watson, Senior Curator, Word & Image Department, Victoria and Albert Museum, London; Douglas Dodds, Head of Central Services, Word & Image Department, Victoria and Albert Museum, London.

Characters

VITO, *eighteen, a quarryman from Carrara*
OLD VITO, *the same man, aged eighty*
LEONARDO, *an artist and inventor*
MICHELANGELO, *an artist*
MACHIAVELLI, *Secretary to the Florentine Republic*
SALAI, *Leonardo's servant and favourite*
SODERINI, *the Gonfaloniere for Life of Florence*
SPINI, *a Commissioner from the Cathedral Works*
PANDOLFINI, *a Consul from the Wool Guild*
LODOVICO, *Michelangelo's father*
ACOLYTES 1 *and* 2, *of the deceased Savonarola*
CONTUCCI, *an artist*

Also
PROWLING MEN, *a North African* WHORE, *Leonardo's*
ENTOURAGE – *among them, a* SINGER, *a* HOODED FIGURE,
and CLERKS, SOLDIERS, MUSICIANS, WORKMEN,
ONLOOKERS, REVELLERS

*The action takes place around a block of marble in Florence,
between 1501 and 1504.*

*This text went to press before the end of rehearsals and may differ
from the play as performed.*

ACT ONE

Prologue

OLD VITO *hunkers in the dappled shade of trees, against a colossal, weathered block of marble, placed horizontally. Aged eighty, he wears the clothes of a mountain quarryman, and speaks with a strong rural accent.*

OLD VITO. I can fly. I know, I know, you look at me now . . . all dry and doddered, the old boy in the shade, the one with the stories . . . you'd never think it, ey, but I can fly. One of them, he promised me this. He said – one day, you will fly. (*Draws a 'V' in the air.*) This shape . . . looks like a bird . . . I'm not lettered, but I know this one. 'V'. It's me. Vito. And look . . . (*Draws 'V's higher and higher.*) . . . through the air, through the ages, for all time, with eagles and angels, I'm flying. Let me show you . . .

He gets up and starts to undo his clothes.

Ohh, this isn't as easy as then . . .

He manages to take off his goatskin pelisse and starts on his jerkin.

. . . I'm talking of when I journeyed to the city, the city of palaces, churches and lions – lions, aye – journeyed there to make my fortune. It's not easy, ey, not a sweet thing? We've all tasted it. A new city, a new place. And you know nothing. All you know is now. Now, nowhere, nothing. This is all you know. Everything else is new. It's so very . . . ai! . . .

Struggling to find words, he whistles and clicks his tongue.

I'd been told just two things. Back home – Sandro – he'd been there, been to Florence. He says, number one – be careful. I say why. He says, the Germans – d'you know their word for men who like arse? I say nay. He says Florentines. I say nay! He says aye! And we don't want you coming back Florentined. So you be careful, ey?

Laughs, and takes off his shirt.

I mean, if you did this there, you'd be like the only tree in a town of dogs.

Laughs again, and sits on the marble block to take off his boots.

Sandro, he says, number two – head for the Duomo. There's a stone yard behind it. Maybe you'll find work there. Well, when I got there, the first thing I saw was this . . . (*Touches the marble block.*) And I thought, this is from home, so . . . (*Crosses himself.*) . . . thank you, it's a sign.

Gives up on his boots.

Nay . . . you'll just have to picture the feet.

Drops his breeches. Stands there naked.

You'll fathom it in a . . . uh . . . which hand goes where? . . . aye, nay, wait . . . this is it!

He strikes up the pose of Michelangelo's David.

D'you see now? Ey? Of course he made one or two changes. But you fathom it now, ey? Aye, yaa, you do! Through the ages, for all time, Vito is flying.

A solo voice sings a haunting tune. OLD VITO *proudly holds his pose. Lights change – flying, dreaming time.*

Scene One

Late morning. A pulse of heat. The stone yard belongs to the Commissioners of Cathedral Works. The gate hangs open, and the rough timber walls have missing planks, creating duck-throughs. The huge marble block dominates the space. A figure is asleep against it, wearing a dusty goatskin pelisse, and with a bag of belongings alongside him. Voices are heard off:

SPINI. . . . The first time, the first commission, this was some thirty-five years ago. . .

MICHELANGELO. Yes, yes . . .

SPINI. . . . And then there was another, some ten years later.

MICHELANGELO. . . . Yes, yes. This has been here all my life. I know the stories . . .

They come into view. MICHELANGELO *is young, short, with unwashed hair and beard, a broken nose; a closed, difficult personality. Interviewing him are a Commissioner from the Opera del Duomo,* SPINI – *thin and pedantic – and a Consul from the Arte della Lana,* PANDOLFINI, *older, heavy, not at ease with art and artists.*

. . . And one of them tells how the first commission was meant for the Master himself. But look, it's a colossus, and he was so old by then.

SPINI (*consulting his files*). Nnhhh . . . no. . . that is not in the records.

MICHELANGELO *shrugs, then hurries forward to touch the block.*

MICHELANGELO. And which of those others did this?

PANDOLFINI. Did what?

MICHELANGELO. It's been worked here and here . . .

PANDOLFINI. Oh, I thought that's how it comes out the ground.

MICHELANGELO. Off the cliffs. No, if cut well it comes off clean . . . with staves wetted and swelling till the block cracks free. (*Examining a semi-carved section on one side.*) What was this meant to be?

SPINI. Nnhhh . . . not in the records.

MICHELANGELO *makes a dismissive noise.* SPINI *frowns at him. Meanwhile,* PANDOLFINI *has found the sleeping figure.*

PANDOLFINI (*clapping his hands*). Hey! Shoo! Shoo!

The figure is VITO – *aged eighteen, remarkably beautiful. He scurries to one side, where he hunkers, watching.*

MICHELANGELO (*still examining the block*). The whole is already quite shallow. Yet this work here means there's hardly any room for, for . . . anything.

SPINI. Young man, if this stone is not to your choosing – well, we need waste you no further.

PANDOLFINI. Nor you us.

MICHELANGELO. No, no . . . proceed.

SPINI. Thank you so much. On both previous occasions the commission has been part of the sculptural programme of twelve Old Testament prophets for the Duomo . . . (*Reads from his files*.) . . . 'Nine braccia in height, at the scale of a giant, and in the appearance and name of a prophet, to be placed up on one of the buttresses of Santa Maria del Fiore . . . '

MICHELANGELO. A prophet? I thought it was David.

SPINI. Yes, it's always been David – for some reason.

MICHELANGELO. Oh, is it not in the records?

SPINI *shoots him a look*.

Say they whatever, they have it wrong. David is not a prophet.

PANDOLFINI. What?

MICHELANGELO. He is a king. The second king of Israel. Yes, in the New Testament, Peter calls David a prophet. But the Old Testament itself holds only four books of major prophets and twelve of minor. The major ones are Isaiah, Jeremiah, Ezekiel . . .

PANDOLFINI. You may well know your Scriptures, young man, but I think we should show all respect to these learned records.

SPINI. Or we won't need a prophet to fortell your chances here.

MICHELANGELO *goes silent, chewing his lip*.

So, you say you have something to show us?

MICHELANGELO *sets a small clay maquette on the marble block. Unlike the famous finished statue, this shows David after the fight, with Goliath's head.*

PANDOLFINI. Oh, I like the head – Goliath's head – severed and underfoot, with stone sunk in brow – I always like the head – it's my favourite bit, the head.

MICHELANGELO. And – the rest of it?

SPINI. Tell me, does he have to be naked?

MICHELANGELO. Yes, he does.

SPINI. And why is that?

MICHELANGELO. Because the Book tells us that so he be.
When David elects to meet the champion of the enemy
Philistines, Goliath by name, the giant man of the land of
Gaza, King Saul lends him his own armour – his brass helmet,
his coat of mail, his mighty sword. But David says to Saul, 'I
cannot go with these, for I have not proved them' – he has not
earned the right to wear a warrior's things. And then the Book
tells us, tells us clearly, 'And David put them off him.'

A beat.

SPINI. Is that it?

MICHELANGELO. It is. 'And David put them off him.'

SPINI. But . . . that doesn't mean he's naked.

PANDOLFINI. No, it doesn't – he's probably in his nether
garments.

MICHELANGELO. What – he goes out to fight the champion of
the Philistines in his nether garments?

PANDOLFINI. Why not?

MICHELANGELO. You want me to carve a giant statue of a man
in his nether garments? That'll look heroic. No, no, no! Go
find someone else. There are many artists . . . portrait painters,
tapestry makers . . . many who are eager to show how we live.
Our clothes, houses, towns, fields. But these things are not
important. There is no background, no background. There is
only us. Naked. As at Creation and at Judgement. And this is
what goes out to fight the monster – not strength, but nakedness. Beauty. Blessed beauty.

Pause.

PANDOLFINI. You have passion, young man.

MICHELANGELO. And is passion not a virtue?

SPINI. It may be, it may.

MICHELANGELO. Truth is a virtue too, and in truth, you need to take advice on this block of yours. From someone more expert than even me. It is so old. So . . . unknown. What if there was suddenly a fissure? Or shelling?

PANDOLFINI. Shelling?

MICHELANGELO. Sometimes . . . a harder section over a softer section . . . it can suddenly come away . . .

VITO. There'll be no shelling. No fissures.

VITO approaches again.

PANDOLFINI *and* SPINI. Shoo! Go away!

MICHELANGELO. No. Let him.

VITO (*to* MICHELANGELO). Listen to this . . .

VITO slaps his palm against one end of the block. MICHELANGELO listens at the other end. A tiny echo, almost as if from a tuning fork. MICHELANGELO nods. VITO grins.

He's strong, him.

MICHELANGELO. He's old.

VITO. He's beautiful.

MICHELANGELO. But is he pure inside? (VITO *nods*.) No veins, no shadows? For me, inside, he must be pure.

VITO. And he is. As you shall see when you cut away his quarry skin. Oh, and his crystals . . . ! Small and close and good. Look . . .

Taking a mallet from his belongings, he aims at one corner.

PANDOLFINI *and* SPINI. No . . . !

MICHELANGELO. It's all right – let him.

With one expert blow, VITO *knocks off a small fragment.*

VITO. Oww, look how beautiful he is.

MICHELANGELO *takes the fragment. Examines it closely. Sniffs the dust on his fingers.* VITO *laughs, and passes the fragment to* SPINI *and* PANDOLFINI.

Like a piece of Parmigiano, ey?

VITO *holds it up to the sunlight, showing the translucency round its edges.*

But see. It's stone. And glass too. Ey? It has a light inside.

MICHELANGELO. It has a soul. (*A beat.*) How d'you know all this?

VITO. I'm from Carrara. And it's you – isn't it? You don't remember? You were there to get a block for . . .

MICHELANGELO. No, I don't, I don't. (*Turning his back on* VITO.) Well now . . .

SPINI. Well now indeed, we have several other candidates to meet.

MICHELANGELO. Oh . . . ?

SPINI. So we will, in due time, communicate by letter, and we will, therein and therewith, say if you are among the final nominations . . .

MICHELANGELO. If . . . ?!

SPINI. . . . And – if you are – we will inform you of the appointed day, the day of judgement.

PANDOLFINI (*chuckling*). Ah – 'day of judgement' – ah-hah! You see young man, we know our Scriptures too. Thank you and good day.

They leave. A beat. Then MICHELANGELO *picks up the little clay maquette of David, as if to smash it. He becomes aware of* VITO *still standing behind him.*

VITO. Are you all right?

MICHELANGELO. People who ask that question of strangers are fools.

VITO. But we're not. Strangers. You must remember. Couple years ago. You with us. In the quarries.

MICHELANGELO. Of course I remember. I remember being there. I was choosing the block for Rome. But I don't remember you.

VITO. Hoh – nay – you do! I was the kid. The goat kid, y'say. On the cliffs, I work the edges. The places the others are too feared to go.

MICHELANGELO. They're egg-shells, those edges.

VITO (*whistles in agreement; then:*). You remember the dog – surely?

MICHELANGELO. The dog?

VITO. Work is finished that day. But it's summer and a clear night. So we're not rushing down to town. We have us some bread and wine and songs on the quarry floor. Beautiful. The white mountain up here, the blue sea down there. Now we hear . . . (*Howls.*) . . . high above us. Someone's dog has gone chasing something, and got himself lost. And now he's calling for help. And Sandro the foreman, he says – Hey dog, nighty-night, rest in peace. He knows, we know, the dog does know too – for something up there, he's supper tonight. We all laugh and start packing up and climbing down. And you whisper to me – Shall we save the dog? And so we slip away from the others – you say they mustn't see. And we start climbing. And at first we're calling the dog and laughing, it's like a game . . . oww, it's . . . ! (*Struggling to find words, he clicks his tongue, stamps his feet.*) But now we have to climb over a ridge. It's tricky. But I'm the kid, I know these rocks. I give you my hand. And now . . . all of a sudden . . . I feel how scared you are. I don't understand. We've just been laughing . . .

MICHELANGELO *lowers his head.*

So now we go back. Fast.

A beat.

MICHELANGELO. You've changed.

VITO. Just grown.

MICHELANGELO. Yes.

Pause.

Well . . . God keep you.

MICHELANGELO *starts to leave.*

VITO. But when do I start?

MICHELANGELO. What?

VITO. As we're climbing. Early on. Climbing and laughing. You say, If ever you're in Florence I'll give you work.

MICHELANGELO. I said that?

VITO. So here I am – in Florence.

MICHELANGELO. You've come all the way from Carrara to . . . ?

VITO. To find the man who liked the kid. (MICHELANGELO *looks away.*) And I did. Ey! I find you and now I work for you. When do I start?

MICHELANGELO. But . . . you've got work. Good work.

VITO. Oww nay. We're just poor people. Breaking our backs. Or dying in accidents. Cutting stone from the mountain.

MICHELANGELO. You're cutting marble.

VITO. There! Hear how you say it. 'Marble.' It's like you're saying 'gold'. To us, it's just stone, just rock, just our mountain. To you it's 'marble'. This is why I'm here. A few years in this city and I'll go home a rich man. (*A beat.*) Let me be your apprentice . . . Master.

MICHELANGELO. Look, I'm . . . you're wrong . . . you do blessed work. In a blessed place. Go home.

MICHELANGELO *quickly exits through the gate.* VITO *starts to follow – but* MICHELANGELO *immediately reappears, hurrying across the stage –*

Don't tell them which way I . . .

– And exits via a duck-through. The Savonarola ACOLYTES *enter. Twin-like, aged about twenty, both with emaciated faces, shaven heads, wearing dirty black robes with hoods. They stare at* VITO, *then move closer, whispering a high-speed*

mantra. VITO *tenses. Music is heard coming round the corner. The* ACOLYTES *flee.* VITO *watches them go, baffled. Meanwhile,* SPINI *and* PANDOLFINI *usher in the next candidate –* LEONARDO. *With long hair (no beard yet), he is middle-aged, handsome, fashionably dressed, a superstar – yet imbued with curiosity and gentleness. He has brought along his* ENTOURAGE: MUSICIANS *and* ATTENDANTS. *Among them is his favourite,* SALAI, *a dissolute 21-year-old. While the* MUSICIANS *play, the* ATTENDANTS *invite* SPINI *and* PANDOLFINI *to sit, and serve them wine and cakes.*

LEONARDO. . . . Well, the eye is the chief means by which we can most fully and subtly appreciate the abundant wonders of Nature, and the ear is the second . . . except it only gains importance because it hears the things which the eye sees . . . if you gentlemen had never seen things with your eyes, you would never be able to describe them to the ears of others . . . so the eye, the eye, the eye . . . and so painting of course, painting is clearly the greatest of the Arts . . . now some call painting 'dumb poetry', but then the painter may say of the poet that his art is 'blind painting', and then you must consider which is the more grievous affliction, to be blind or to be dumb? . . . and in this eternal war between the painter and the poet, only one thing is sure – the painter's gift is certainly less tedious to receive.

His ENTOURAGE *laugh. As* LEONARDO *takes breath:*

SPINI. Pardon me, Master . . .

PANDOLFINI. Honoured Master.

SPINI. . . . Honoured, honoured – it is indeed a privilege to hear you discourse on these matters, but we wonder if we could perhaps turn our attention to the sculpture of this block?

LEONARDO. Sculpture? Ah me – now we're ducking low. (*The* ENTOURAGE *laugh.*) Sculpture? This is of course a purely mechanical exercise, a stonemason's craft, and . . . Oh! . . . it is accompanied by a great sweat which mixes with the marble dust and forms a kind of mud over the face, and then this dust flows all over the poor man so that now he looks like a baker . . .

PANDOLFINI (*whispering to* SPINI). Does he want this commission?

LEONARDO. . . . And his back is covered with a mess of chips, and his house is made filthy with the snowstorm of the stone, and noisy with the bang of the hammer, the slam and the bang, the bang-bang-bang, the bi-bam-bam . . .

LEONARDO *starts to improvise a song, jotting down the tune in his notebook. The* MUSICIANS *play along quietly. Meanwhile,* SALAI *sits next to* SPINI *and* PANDOLFINI, *and smiles his sly smile.*

SALAI. Ah no, don't worry, this is simply his way of starting.

SPINI. Starting? Does he, as it were, realise why we're here?

SALAI. Oh yes, ah ti-ta-tu.

PANDOLFINI. Yet he doesn't seem that keen on sculpture.

SALAI. No, but he'll do it.

SPINI. Do it?

SALAI. If you ask sweetly.

PANDOLFINI. What?

SALAI (*rubbing his fingers together*). He'll do anything . . . y'know.

PANDOLFINI *and* SPINI. What?!

SALAI. Go on – take him aside, name your fee, and he'll do it. It'll save us all hours and hours of . . . (*Indicates* LEONARDO*'s performance.*) . . . di-diggili-dee.

PANDOLFINI. Pardon me, but who are you?

SALAI. I'm his voice. His real voice.

SPINI. We've had the eye, the ear, and now we have the voice.

SALAI. Mm-mn.

PANDOLFINI. Yes, well, your voice is not pleasing to our ear, young man.

SALAI. Then I must change it. Here you have one of the most renowned men in Italy. All Italy. Not just in Milan, in Rome, the other states. Who's more renowned in all Italy? Him in the Vatican – the joke in the cope? So wouldn't it be an honour – no, la-li-la, a great fortune for Florence to have this man carve their giant?

SPINI *and* PANDOLFINI *exchange a look, then confer in whispers.*

SPINI (*to* SALAI). Please tell him that we will communicate by letter, and disclose whether he's among the final nomi . . . (PANDOLFINI *whispers again.*) Ah, yes, no. . . tell him, ask him, please, to return here this time next week, which will be, in fact, the day of judgement.

PANDOLFINI *chuckles: 'Day of judgement.'*

And now if you'll make our apologies – the pressures of office, you know – and we'll just . . . go.

They exit swiftly, bowing to LEONARDO. *He stops the music.*

LEONARDO. What's happened?

SALAI. They've gone, Master.

LEONARDO. Gone? But . . . I was entertaining them . . . perhaps teasing a little, but . . . gone? (*Angry.*) What did you say to them?

SALAI. I said they should just ask you, and you'll do it, their commission. But in truth it's you who should ask them! (*Banging the marble block.*) You could have this. The right word in the right ear, and for absolute sure – this is yours. But no, you won't fight for this. No . . . 'I'm not asking them, let them ask me, I am the Master, the Master of Remarkable Fame and . . . '

LEONARDO. Fame? Fame! You think I'd boast of fame?! That great ugly bird – every claw is a knife, a bleeding knife, every feather is a tongue, a blabbing tongue. You think I honour fame?

SALAI. I think you prize it and despise it, but I think you prize it more.

LEONARDO *goes silent, and pats scent onto his neck.*

And you know what else I think, my darla? Fame is like beauty – look away, look back, it's gone. You want fame to stay fresh, darla, you must keep fighting, fighting!

LEONARDO *takes out his notebook and jots notes about a tiny insect on the ground, writing from right to left.* SALAI *gives a signal. The* MUSICIANS *play, the* ENTOURAGE *clear up, and then exit.* SALAI *stays.* VITO *– wolfing down leftover food – watches* LEONARDO *sketching.*

VITO. What are you doing?

LEONARDO. Hmn? Look at the wing, the leg joint, the spur . . . isn't this a fine piece of design, of miniature construction? . . . man could never make this . . . he can make gods by the handful, but never one of these. Now tell me . . . who are you?

VITO. Vito. Vito Barattini. Of Carrara.

LEONARDO. Ah . . . (*Indicates the marble block.*) . . . you're related.

VITO (*laughing*). And you – who are you?

LEONARDO (*hesitates, then:*). Here's one.

VITO. One what?

LEONARDO. A kind of riddle.

VITO. All right.

LEONARDO. Easy or hard?

VITO. Easy.

LEONARDO. In the highest regions of the air, serpents will be seen fighting with birds.

VITO. What . . . like when storks catch snakes?

LEONARDO. Like that exactly.

VITO. Ey! 'S too easy. C'mon!

LEONARDO. Very well. Men will be treated with great ceremony – without their knowledge.

VITO. Uh. Don't know. Nay, wait. Is it like when they're asleep or . . . dead? Is it like funerals?

LEONARDO. It is like funerals exactly. You're good.

VITO (*laughs*). More.

LEONARDO (*smiles*). Later.

SALAI *watches them intently.*

So – Vito – did you see my interview for the commission?

VITO. I did.

LEONARDO. And what do you think?

VITO. I think, mayhap, you missed your chance.

LEONARDO. I think, mayhap, I did.

LEONARDO *roars with laughter.* VITO *joins in.* SALAI *steps in.*

SALAI. No – you didn't. They said, with you, Master, there's simply no need for the usual procedures.

LEONARDO. What . . . what does that mean . . . are they giving it to me?

SALAI. The true question, Master, is how can they not give it to you?

LEONARDO. Hmn.

SALAI. And in the meantime, Master, we have other people to see . . .

LEONARDO (*rising*). We do, we do.

SALAI. . . . Other commissions to consider.

LEONARDO. We have, we have. (*To* VITO.) There you are, y'see . . . one missed chance allows ten others to land . . . there's so much, so much . . . look, think . . . what is it like to be bread as it's baked, or soil being tilled, and . . . what of the spine of a snake, the spark of a firefly, the tongue of a wood-pecker? Think of these things. There's so much! (*Indicates the marble block.*) This fall of light here, this shape of sun and shadow . . . why does it strike me as so beautiful? The way the old stone seems to receive the new light, to know it . . . and I know it too, somehow, though I've never even glanced here before . . . yet it makes me feel . . . a kind of pity, a kind of peace. Why? (*Staring intently at* VITO.) What exactly is beauty . . . d'you see?

VITO. Uh . . .

SALAI. Master!

LEONARDO. Yes, we must, we must. (*To* SALAI.) My creature, my bat, my devil, my ningle . . . is there not a carnival in the city tonight? (SALAI *nods*.) Good, good, then we must join the revels . . . if I have missed my chance, we must celebrate it, and if I have not, and won the commission, that too is cause for celebration.

LEONARDO *exits*. SALAI *hangs back, looking at* VITO *coldly. Then he brings out a few coins.*

SALAI. Is this acceptable . . . for the night . . . the whole night?

VITO. What?! I'm not a, a, a . . . ! Go, boy, go with your kim kams! I know about you here, ey? I know about 'Florentines'.

SALAI. Do you? I doubt it. But come, Mister Carrara, Mister Big Rock, come and sport with us tonight. Nothing will happen to you that you don't want, I give you my word. And, as you will find, I may do many bad deeds – and oh, darla, I can be very, very bad – but there's one sure thing about me – I always tell the truth. (VITO *takes the coins cautiously*.) Let's see you back here at midnight. Keep yourself clean till then.

He exits. VITO *hears voices coming round the corner again:*

SPINI. . . . The first commission, thirty-five years ago, part of the sculptural programme for the Duomo, asks for a figure nine braccia in height, to be placed up on one of the buttresses of . . .

SPINI *and* PANDOLFINI *lead the next candidate to the marble block – the artist* CONTUCCI, *a thin, nervous man – while* OLD VITO *emerges from the shaded side of the yard, dressed as we first saw him.*

OLD VITO. Giants. In the mountains, we tell of a giant so high
   his head is in the clouds. He can't see up there, so he has his
   eyes on his feet. On the heels. So he only sees what he's
   already passed. (*Laughs*.) There are some men like that, ey?
   Their brains work in the heavens, their legs chew up the earth,
   and us – you and me – they leave us in the dust behind them.
   What makes some men grow like that, ey? Don't know, go ask
   a wiser skull than mine. (*Swaggering*.) But by the end of that
   first day in Florence . . . and I didn't know this at the time . . .
   but me – Vito Barattini of Carrara – only here one day and I'd
   already made me mates with two of these giant men. And then
   – Holy Mother – another one! A giant of government. Let's
   call him the Prince . . . the prince of politicians . . .

The lights change around him.

Scene Two

Dusk. Noise of crowds gathering, singing. MACHIAVELLI *runs
on; he has beady eyes, and a small permanent smile.* Young VITO
watches from the shadows. MACHIAVELLI *is leading a North
African* WHORE.

MACHIAVELLI. . . . Say nothing. Stay veiled. Don't look at me.
   You don't know me. This isn't happening . . . (*He begins
   sodomising her.*) And let's be brisk . . . I have an appointment
   . . . tighter, tighter . . . tsk! . . . no, this isn't really . . . (*He sees*
   VITO.) Here, boy. Watch. Good. (*To the* WHORE.) Tighter,
   tighter . . . (*She puts out her hand. He pays.*) Ah good, better
   . . . (*To* VITO.) Watch . . . show me you're watching . . . (*To
   them both.*) Good . . . and better . . . and best . . . and . . .

Voices and flamelight are approaching.

. . . Perfect!

All in one, he finishes, and dismisses both the WHORE *and*
VITO.

. . . Thank you so much, be off . . .

As several figures enter:

. . . Now there's timing.

Arriving from one side is the Gonfaloniere, SODERINI *– aristocratic, affable, indecisive – signing documents with a* CLERK, *while appearing from the other side are* SPINI *and* PANDOLFINI.

SODERINI. I haven't got long.

MACHIAVELLI. Who has, Excellency?

SODERINI (*listening to the crowds*). What is going on tonight?

MACHIAVELLI. Some kind of carnival, Excellency – we haven't licensed it, but it seems that the people are celebrating the fall of Milan to the French.

SODERINI. Oh, good. Good for them. Good for the people!

SPINI (*quietly to* PANDOLFINI). Ohhh, all those wild fires again . . . that wild hurling of stones.

PANDOLFINI . Ohhh, let us lock ourselves in when this is done.

SODERINI *finishes signing documents, and the* CLERK *exits.* SODERINI *nudges the marble block with his foot.*

SODERINI. So this is it?

MACHIAVELLI. This is indeed it, Excellency.

SODERINI. This old thing?

PANDOLFINI. My feelings exactly, Excellency. I can picture it being cut into a good marble floor or a couple of sturdy pillars, but . . . a giant? At any rate, if we finally get the job done this time, at least it'll clear some space round here.

SODERINI. It certainly will. (*Contemplating the block.*) What is it that artists can see, d'you think, Secretary?

MACHIAVELLI. Oh I don't think they see exactly, Excellency . . . I think they know a kind of dreaming, enjoy a kind of intoxication, suffer a kind of madness.

SODERINI. Hh! Just imagine trying to govern a state of artists.

MACHIAVELLI. Oh impossible, Excellency. The streets would
    be filled with jabber and nakedness, time would run backwards,
    and chickens would go to war with eggs. (*Everyone laughs.*) In
    the meanwhile, Excellency, and with reference to this block,
    these good gentlemen, meeting together with their colleagues
    at, respectively, the Opera del Duomo and the Arte della Lana,
    have narrowed our choice down to three . . . (*Presenting sepa-
    rate sheets of paper.*) Number One is . . . well, let's call him the
    Young One . . .

SODERINI. Mmn.

MACHIAVELLI. Number Two is . . .

SODERINI. Ah!

MACHIAVELLI. Exactly – the Famous One. And Number Three
    is . . .

SODERINI. No, don't think I've heard of him.

MACHIAVELLI. No, but the Reliable One, Excellency.

PANDOLFINI. He'd be my choice, sir. A good craftsman, a . . .

SODERINI. No doubt, no doubt, but, with respect, if we can have
    Number Two, why should we bother with One or Three?

MACHIAVELLI. Gentlemen?

SPINI (*consulting notes*). Number Two, Excellency, for all his
    fame and his gifts, is not known as a great finisher.

SODERINI. Finisher?

PANDOLFINI. He has only recently returned to Florence,
    Excellency . . . in fact as one of the refugees fleeing the
    sacking of Milan.

SODERINI. He was in Milan . . . ?!

SPINI. Where he'd been commissioned, as it happens, to sculpt a
    giant. An equestrian giant. This was only ever made in clay,
    never cast in its bronze, and has ended up being used by the
    invading French, by their archers, as target practice.

SODERINI. But . . . the original commission . . . this was for
    the Sforzas?!

MACHIAVELLI. Oh yes, but we mustn't hold that against him, Excellency . . . nor that Number One, the Young One, was first in the employ of the Medicis here in Florence and then the cardinals of the Borgia Pope in Rome. And I fear it is the Borgias we will have to watch next. (*As* SODERINI *groans:*) No, but you see, Excellency, artists serve at the foot of the great god Necessity – they must sell their skills to anyone who can pay. Even with the finest works we know, adorning our cathedrals and piazzas, works which can cause us to tilt back our heads in an ecstasy of devotion . . . it is always worth remembering that we are simply enjoying the exertions of some hard-jobbing whore.

SODERINI. Ah well – not really my territory then, Secretary. (*They laugh.* SPINI *and* PANDOLFINI *shift uneasily.*) And while we're on the subject, these three candidates – are any of them sodomites?

MACHIAVELLI. Surely that's the wrong question, Excellency. This is Florence. Are any of them not?

SODERINI. I'm serious.

MACHIAVELLI. Of course you are, Excellency, pray pardon.

SODERINI. It comes up in meeting after meeting with the Signoria – how all of Europe is laughing at us. And now with an important commission like this, and with a dangerous subject. Y'know . . . David. Y'know . . . the nakedness.

SPINI. I couldn't agree more, Excellency. The nakedness is dangerous indeed. Even our great deceased Master, in his renowned bronze of David, even he exceeded himself – in my humble view. I mean, the feather. The feather on the helmet of Goliath's severed head. Did it really have to go all the way up the boy's inner thigh? I mean, did it really have to touch, almost stroke, the boy's little . . .

SODERINI. Yes, thank you. But this new statue – it is definitely David and Goliath, isn't it? What I mean is, it's not . . . David and Jonathan?

SPINI. God save us!

SODERINI. Exactly.

PANDOLFINI. Excellency, I'm no expert at all – good Lord no, I'm from the Wool Guild – but apparently this block, although appearing huge to us, is in fact rather shallow for a figure of David. I don't believe there is room for Jonathan as well.

MACHIAVELLI. Except in one position.

SODERINI. Secretary!

MACHIAVELLI. Yes, forgive me, Excellency, please let us blame the night and the revels. Come now, to business. So . . . (*To* SPINI *and* PANDOLFINI.) These candidates of yours – any of them sodomites?

SPINI. Well, we did, in fact, take the precaution of checking with the Officers of the Night, and were given leave to examine their records. (*Consulting notes.*) No evidence for the Young One, and it's unlikely – he's fiercely devout.

MACHIAVELLI. Ah, one of those – drunk with God.

SPINI. But as for the Famous One, it is my duty to inform you that, yes, he was arrested on a sodomy charge.

SODERINI *and* MACHIAVELLI. Really . . . ?!

SPINI. This was many years ago. He was only twenty-four, still an apprentice . . . he and three companions were charged with the sodomy, possible rape, of one, Jacopo Saltarelli, seventeen years old . . . the charge seemed serious . . . and sodomitic rape can of course incur burning at the stake . . . but after two hearings, the case was, mysteriously, dropped.

SODERINI. And nowadays?

SPINI. Nowadays, although still surrounded by a little gaggle of exquisites, he is reputed to be celibate.

Pause.

SODERINI. And the Reliable One?

SPINI. Oh no, no – he's wed, with children.

MACHIAVELLI. There's our sodomite then.

SODERINI. Secretary . . . ! (*Breaks into laughter.*) All right, so which of these 'whores' will you have? The Young One, the Famous One, the Reliable One?

MACHIAVELLI. Well, come, come, we're a Republic, we must take a vote – gentlemen?

PANDOLFINI (*holding up his hand*). Reliable.

SPINI (*holding up his hand*). Famous.

SODERINI (*holding up his hand*). Famous . . . or Reliable.

MACHIAVELLI (*holding up his hand*). Cheapest. (*Everyone laughs.*) But let's not decide, let's not say, let's think on it, and meet again.

SODERINI. Very good, and so, where do I have to be next . . . ?

MACHIAVELLI *leads out* SODERINI, *while* SPINI *and* PANDOLFINI *also exit. The yard's timber walls creak, and* PROWLING MEN *start drifting back and forth past* VITO. *Fireworks illuminate the scene. The* PROWLING MEN *jump into the shadows, while* VITO *finds the Savonarola* ACOLYTES *next to him.*

ACOLYTE 1. Calm.

ACOLYTE 2. Calm, calm.

ACOLYTE 1. We know what you are.

ACOLYTE 2. We know what you do.

ACOLYTE 1. We did it once too.

ACOLYTE 2. We worked as lumps of meat.

ACOLYTE 1 *and* 2. Lumps of meat, meat with eyes.

VITO. Meat with eyes . . . ?

ACOLYTE 1. Until he saved us.

ACOLYTE 2. God's Jaws, God's Jaws.

ACOLYTE 1. Saved all the boy meat in the city.

ACOLYTE 2. Boy meat, boy meat.

VITO. Ey, wait! I'm not a . . .

ACOLYTE 1. And made us into an army . . .

ACOLYTE 2. . . . . Of angels and avengers . . .

ACOLYTE 1. . . . His army . . .

ACOLYTE 1 *and* 2. . . . The Friar's Youth!

They open their robes. Underneath is an odd white garment, part soldier's uniform, part choirboy's shift. A blood red cross hangs from their necks. An explosion of fireworks. They look up.

ACOLYTE 1. This is what the sky was like when we burnt them . . .

ACOLYTE 2. . . . Books, paintings, wigs, mirrors . . .

ACOLYTE 1 *and* 2. . . . Vanities, not necessities!

Another, bigger flash of fireworks.

ACOLYTE 1. And this is what it was like when they burnt him . . .

ACOLYTE 2. . . . God's Jaws, God's Jaws.

ACOLYTE 1. God's Jaws, Christ's voice . . .

ACOLYTE 2. . . . Christ's voice on earth.

ACOLYTE 1. And what did Rome do?

ACOLYTE 2. Rome stopped it.

ACOLYTE 1. Stopped his voice, broke his body, and he was . . .

ACOLYTE 1 *and* 2 (*with violent grief*). . . . Burnt!

ACOLYTE 1. Yet he lives on.

ACOLYTE 1 *and* 2. In us, in us.

ACOLYTE 1. Join us now.

ACOLYTE 2. On this night of sin . . .

They grab VITO. *He breaks free.*

VITO. Look, I'm not . . . ! Just . . . just . . . (*He growls, stamps, claps his hands: 'Go away!'*)

ACOLYTE 1 (*to* ACOLYTE 2). He will come to us.

ACOLYTE 2 (*to* VITO). You will come to us . . .

Voices are heard from the darkness – 'There they are!', 'Go burn on your own bonfires!', 'Try and stop our hailstones now!' – and a whooping gang of stone-throwing REVELLERS arrive, unleashing a storm of missiles. As the ACOLYTES flee for their lives, VITO ducks behind the marble block. Stillness. VITO's head peers out nervously. He listens. A lion roars.

VITO (*to himself*). And what in God's good land is that?!

Fireworks explode. The lights change.

Scene Three

Midnight. The revels are at full tilt. At the marble block the PROWLING MEN are moving back and forth hungrily, while VITO tries to avoid any direct touch. Now a fantastical moon appears above. The PROWLING MEN start to flee.

LEONARDO (*off*). Oh no, gentlemen, please don't go, this is for you . . . your nights are, alas, often quite grey . . . let us colour this one for you . . .

The MEN watch from the shadows. Music starts – a wailing and beating of primitive instruments. LEONARDO's ENTOURAGE enter, dressed as Greek gods. A heady, drugged atmosphere. VITO is fed a potion, which he enjoys. Now LEONARDO appears – the only one who's sober – keenly watching and sketching.

THE SINGER.
     The King of Gods
     Imperial Jove
     Burned with fierce desire,
     One Ganymede
     A Trojan boy
     His heart and blood doth fire.

SALAI has entered as Jove, while anonymous hands change VITO into Ganymede, a young shepherd from ancient times, with chiton, straw hat, and crook.

Not swan nor dove
Nor ocean's gull
Would suit God's purposed aim,
A Noblebird
He chose and thus
An eagle he became.

SALAI *(as Jove) transforms into a colossal eagle.*

This mighty eagle cleft the air
With bold, vast-lying wings,
And like thunderbolts
Towards the earth
The love of Jove he brings.

The eagle descends on VITO. *He tries to defend himself with his crook.*

And there amid
The Phrygian groves
New pleasures to enjoy . . .

The eagle swoops with increased force, and lifts VITO *off the ground.*

He stole away
He stole away
He stole away the boy!

The group create the Rape of Ganymede. It quickly grows out of control. SALAI*'s talons scratch at* VITO, *and tear away half of his chiton. The* ATTENDANTS *join in, groping* VITO. *The* MEN *in the shadows stamp and pant – they want to see real sex.* VITO *fights his way free – a powerful country lad against effeminate city boys.*

VITO *(throwing stones left by the* REVELLERS*).* Here – taste – these scorplings – here – you rubbish – bite on these!

The ATTENDANTS *scatter. The* MEN *flee.* VITO *corners* SALAI.

Ey! You gave me your word – you said you tell the truth.

SALAI. I did, I do. I promised you wouldn't do anything you didn't want. And so? That's what we were giving you.

VITO *attacks* SALAI *again.* LEONARDO *intervenes, pulling* VITO *to a safe corner (where he changes back into his clothes), and grabbing* SALAI.

LEONARDO. Come here! I thought you said he agreed.

SALAI. He did. He just doesn't know he did. Mister Carra', Mister Big Rock – I know her kind – I can smell her kind – and there's not one of them, these big, cunt-rutting stallions, none of them who don't think about it the other way round!

LEONARDO. Oh, why do you always have to be . . . you? (*Slapping him.*) You . . . you . . . you!

SALAI. Ai Master, na-na-na . . . !

LEONARDO (*to* VITO). You must pardon us if there's been confusion . . . no, not if . . . there is confusion . . . in us all . . . him, me, you, everyone . . . confusion between us and our flesh. Lust is an infection, a dirty itch we are born with, and must live with, but it is of course repellent. The sexing organs are especially repellent, they put us on the level of beasts, and . . . Oh! . . . were it not for the beauty of our other features – above these organs – why, no one would mate at all, and Nature would lose the human species!

SALAI (*nursing his wounds*). Mh-hh? So why this story – why Ganymede – why do we do it again and again, with all those other boys before? What happens while you're watching us? My oyster. What do you do with your dirty itch?

LEONARDO. By my blood, let me make us a new machine – a tongue clamp.

SALAI. You'll never clamp me, my dilling, I'm too full of your secrets, I'll puff up and blow, and then the whole world will see them . . .

LEONARDO. Shush! What's the matter with you? Go home.

SALAI *starts to stride off.*

Wait! (*Indicates* VITO.) First ask pardon of him.

SALAI. I can't, Master – I have to shush.

He exits, followed by the ENTOURAGE.

LEONARDO. I don't know what to do with him, I truly don't . . .
and I've been saying that for years . . . I got him in Milan . . .
he was just ten, a little pretty boy, but odd. I named him Salai
from the start, 'Little Devil' . . . he supped for two and made
havoc for four. And nowadays, he . . . well, as a little devil
should, he sits on my shoulder and tells me the truth. (*Pause.*)
I love him, you see.

VITO *snorts*.

No – not like that! (*Waves his notebook.*) I may watch them, yes,
I study them, but I do not participate. Very well . . . goodnight.

He starts to go.

VITO. Ey! Nay, wait, wait, wait. It's not just 'goodnight', ey?
What was that about?

LEONARDO. What was what about?

VITO. 'What was what . . . ' Ey boy – go bottle your farts! You
ask, 'What was . . . ' I'm up in the mad air and . . . and this
mad thing is . . . !

He stamps on the eagle costume, abandoned on the ground.

LEONARDO. Peace, peace. What is the matter with everyone
tonight? Listen to me . . .

VITO *rushes at* LEONARDO *and grabs him.*

VITO. Nay, you listen. And listen good. You don't treat me like
that, ey? Nobody treats me like that. I am Vito Barattini of
Carrara. And nobody treats Vito Barattini of Carrara like that.
D'you see? So you tell me now – what was that about?

LEONARDO (*flustered*). It's just . . . some costumes and
machines left over from Milan . . . when we were employed at
the Castello Sforzesco. . . we did masques there . . .

VITO. And what's a masque? What's it for?

LEONARDO. Well, it's a . . . a kind of art.

VITO. And what's that for?

LEONARDO. Look . . . it's very simple, a masque is . . . it's for
. . . amusement, relaxation . . . when work is done, and . . .

VITO. Oh? Oh! Where I come from, when work is done, you climb down the mountain. It takes hours. When you get home, you sleep. When you wake, you climb up the mountain again. This takes even longer. Then you work. And when you're not working or climbing, you do two things. You eat and you sleep. And maybe fuck if you're not too tired. D'you see what I'm saying? You eat and sleep – so you can climb and work. You fuck – so you can get young who can start climbing and working too. These things – you know what they're for. See what I'm saying? Aye, nay, you don't, you can't. Oh man, just go make you a masque!

VITO *starts to exit*.

LEONARDO. You're a philosopher, Vito Barattini of Carrara . . . and you're right . . . no doubt I'll wake tomorrow and think of all the other things I might've done with today. So you must pardon me – pardon me, please.

VITO. D'y'know what? You make me feel . . . ai! . . . like uhh . . . (*Clicks his tongue, snaps his fingers, expressing how strange* LEONARDO *is.* LEONARDO *watches.* VITO *becomes self-conscious.*) Aye well. Up there. Up the cliffs, the scars, the quarries. There you can't always use words. There you must also use calls, clicks, whistles, songs. Oh, and the echo. You must use the echo.

LEONARDO. It holds power, I think, this place, your Carrara . . . listen to the very word . . . Car-ra-ra . . . you can hear it . . . iron hitting stone.

VITO. Aye well. The work is hard. But the place is beautiful. (*Pause.*) You from here?

LEONARDO. Not really . . . I'm a country boy like you . . . of the land, like you . . . that great book, the Land, greater than Knowledge, and open to us all . . . though only a few can read it . . . wouldn't you say?

VITO. Don't know . . . maybe . . . aye.

LEONARDO. Aye. It's about a day's ride, the place where I was born . . . but tiny, tiny . . . on top of a hill.

VITO. Is it beautiful?

LEONARDO. No. Much more than beautiful. There is an old road, a lovely old stone road which runs down from this tiny . . . it's hardly even a village . . . down into the town, down to Vinci, and in May when the wild poppies open among the olive groves . . . red flowers, silver trees . . . and the earth's just beginning to bake, still smelling sweet . . . marigolds, fennel, cut hay . . . and the air's clean, fresh, like it's washed, almost like sea air . . . and it's very high, this road, so high that birds are flying below you . . . no, this place is not beautiful, it is paradise.

VITO *stares at him, fascinated.*

Paradise . . . and I was given a blessing there . . . truly . . . I was blessed by a bird, a kite, which landed on my cradle . . . this is my first memory . . . a golden eagle bird, yet I felt no fear, only wonder . . . and it blessed me like this, with its feathers against my lips . . . like this . . . (*Brushes his fingers across* VITO*'s lips.*) And from then on, as I grew and began to walk that lovely road, and saw birds flying – below me – I had this . . . a strange sense of falling – at first I would catch hold of bushes, branches – my balance! – what's happening? – and then I began to enjoy it, to will it on . . . let me fall, let me fall further, faster, into this view, into the sky . . . can you imagine! . . . the tops of trees below you, those great slopes of pine and laurel, the tall cypresses rising like spires . . . and you're above them! . . . imagine . . . listen . . . right round your ears, you can hear the air – air, not wind – it's not moving – you are. Surely it's possible. It's what your heart already does when you walk that road – surely your body can do it too. Fly.

LEONARDO *crouches alongside the eagle costume.*

It just needs . . . I don't know . . . you're good at riddles . . . help me to solve this one, the riddle of flight . . . probably so simple, that balance, that weight, that bird's wing, just out of reach . . . what do you think?

VITO (*laughing*). Uh. Dunno. Maybe it's something we can grow. Hair like a cloak. Or a new kind of skin, like bats have.

LEONARDO. Bats, good, yes, flying fish, dragonflies, yes . . . creatures who've escaped their own element . . . who've had that privilege . . . Like you too, you're a country fox in these city streets, you'll help me to sniff it out, hm? (*Demonstrates with the eagle costume.*) You see these giant limbs, with their giant fingers . . . in still air, they move at, say, six degrees of velocity . . . a wind against them will take, say, two away . . . but at four they can keep moving yet . . . it's a question of support you see, the percussion of these wings . . . but do we possess enough strength in our own arms? Is it like this . . . like swimming in water?

VITO. Or rowing . . . is it like this?

LEONARDO *and* VITO *are close, almost touching.*

LEONARDO. Or . . . is it something quite else . . . a sail, a machine? . . . I don't know . . . but I will . . . I will fly with those birds. And you will too.

Fireworks explode – causing the lions to roar.

VITO. What is that?!

LEONARDO. It's from the Via dei Leoni . . . the lion-pit . . . they're the symbol of our city, the Marzocco. . . I'll take you there, my fox, I'll show you the lions, I'll show you everything . . .

SALAI (*off*). Master.

LEONARDO *quickly moves away from* VITO. SALAI *ushers in a* HOODED FIGURE.

SALAI. This man was waiting at home. He says he's been waiting for hours. He says he's from the Duke at Imola . . . (LEONARDO *goes still;* SALAI *whispers:*) . . . The spawn of the Pope, the Borgia bastard.

LEONARDO *takes the* HOODED FIGURE *to one side.*

(*To* VITO.) I'm so sorry – eh? Sorry you didn't get to see the rest of the Ganymede story. You want to know what happens? So once they're back in Olympus, Jove makes Ganymede his very special boy, his cup bearer. So naturally Jove's wife, Juno, she hates his deepest guts, she wants to kill him. So then Jove makes him immortal – he's Aquarius, look, up there – and now she can't touch him. So you know what she does, my darla? She kills his kin instead, his earthly kith 'n' kin, all of them, massacred. Isn't that a sad story, darla, showing what happens when a boy gets between a man and his wife. You got any kith 'n' kin, darla? Back in old Carrara? Because we have associates in that region, close associates, all a bit funny like me, all a bit, y'know, miaow-miaow, muggler-muggler. And they tell me the rock slides in those mountains, they're just . . . ooh, horribilis! You must fret about your kith 'n' kin, darla, hmmn?

VITO *is scared. Now* LEONARDO *ushers over the* HOODED FIGURE.

LEONARDO (*to* SALAI). Give him food and bed – the best – and stable his horse – he needs to ride back tomorrow.

SALAI *exits with the* HOODED FIGURE. LEONARDO *gives a grim laugh.*

VITO. What?

LEONARDO. I've been offered another commission . . . only it's as military engineer . . . to the most ferocious warlord in the land, and . . . I detest war, but . . . well, the fee is tremendous. So now if I don't fight for this piece of stone . . . ! (*He kicks at the marble block.*) All right, here's one.

VITO. One what?

LEONARDO. Easy or hard?

VITO. Oh, uh . . .

LEONARDO. A man can fight with stone or fight with steel, so what shall he do?

VITO. What does he want to do?

LEONARDO. What does he want to do? He wants to fly.

LEONARDO *exits fast.*

VITO. Wait – I don't know your name . . . !

But he's gone. VITO *is left alone, listening to the lions. Fireworks illuminate their prowling shadows.* VITO *watches in awe.* OLD VITO *comes forward.*

OLD VITO. He took me to see them the next day. I'd never seen lions before. And nay, boy, I was all on gog! They're . . . they're . . . (*Swings his arms, stamps, trying to express himself.*) . . . they're . . . lions! I mean, at home, we'd heard about lions. In the Bible. The Lion of Judah, Daniel in the lion's den, and the like. But this was what lions look like. So . . . David . . .

VITO (*touching the marble block*). . . . . David.

OLD VITO. . . . . We'd heard about him too in the Bible. But what would he look like?

The lions roar. Lights change.

Scene Four

The roaring of lions grows into a tremendous rumbling, creaking noise.

OLD VITO. On the eve of the appointed day, the day of judge-ment, there was a mighty sight to be seen. The giant stood up.

The marble block is being winched into an upright position. ONLOOKERS have gathered to watch – around and on top of the yard's timber walls – everyone singing an anthem of exal-tation. There's heavy mist in the air, mixing with years of dust which stream off the block. Lowered into a scaffold cage with a turntable floor, it settles with a boom. The ONLOOKERS drift away. Only MICHELANGELO appears to be left – with young VITO watching from one side. But now, as the dust clears, the Savonarola ACOLYTES step forward. They open their robes, revealing the white uniforms and red crosses.

MICHELANGELO (*glancing round anxiously*). What do you want?

ACOLYTE 1. You.

ACOLYTE 2. You, you.

MICHELANGELO. What?

ACOLYTE 1. He's coming back.

ACOLYTE 2. God's Jaws, God's Jaws.

ACOLYTE 1. You followed him.

MICHELANGELO. I did not follow him! I went to some of the sermons. Thousands of people went . . .

ACOLYTE 1. And followed him.

ACOLYTE 2. Like you did.

ACOLYTE 1. Now lead us.

ACOLYTE 2. To meet him again.

MICHELANGELO. What? He's dead.

ACOLYTE 1. Not his words, not his teachings.

ACOLYTE 2. God's Jaws are working again.

ACOLYTE 1. Help people hear them again.

ACOLYTE 2. Come away from all this.

ACOLYTE 1. Think. None of this. Not just no vanities . . .

ACOLYTE 2. . . . Not just no jewels, no wigs, no mirrors, but . . .

ACOLYTE 1 *and* 2. . . . No art at all.

MICHELANGELO. What? No! If the art is from the Bible it can be . . .

ACOLYTE 1 *and* 2. Heresy.

> MICHELANGELO *goes silent*. ACOLYTE 1 *moves in, changing tack*.

ACOLYTE 1. There is no equivocation. The second command-ment allows no equivocation. 'Thou shalt not make thee any graven image . . . '

MICHELANGELO. . . . Of Him, of God, no graven image of . . .

ACOLYTE 1. No – not just of God. There's no equivocation –
'Thou shalt not make thee any graven image or any likeness of any thing that is in Heaven above or that is in the earth beneath or that is in the waters beneath the earth. Thou shalt not bow

down thyself to them and thou shalt not serve them.' Thus
sayeth the second commandment. You know your Scriptures,
you know it is true. No equivocation.

MICHELANGELO. You people speak the language of No, of
Not. But I say yes, yes – make a graven image, yes, if it be a
window to Heaven, yes, if it shows that God and His great
cloud of witnesses are present, on hand, on high, yes! And yes,
if it shows the spark that lit Heaven when God touched Adam,
casting Man in His own likeness – yes! It's so simple, so hard,
so perfect – what I see – and what must be shown – just one
blinding thing. Man. Yes.

ACOLYTE 1. Well yes – yes of course – yes, Satan snarls many
in his bonds, many who worship the creature in place of the
Creator.

ACOLYTE 2. The creature in place of the Creator.

MICHELANGELO. No. That's not what I mean. I mean that
art is . . .

ACOLYTE 1. The only art in man is Faith.

ACOLYTE 2. The great gift in man is Faith.

MICHELANGELO. No! I mean . . . yes! But you can also. . .

ACOLYTE 1 *and* 2. Faith is our only gift!

MICHELANGELO. No. . . please no. (*Glances round.*) Oh this is
madness. Tomorrow is a day of days for me. Yet before it even
dawns, you'll get me banished from this city, and you'll get
yourselves . . .

ACOLYTE 1. We'll get what he got.

ACOLYTE 2. The great sacrifice, the great honour . . .

ACOLYTES 1 *and* 2. . . . . Eternity, ecstacy – martyrdom!

*They open their robes to reveal secret pockets – with little
phials of ash.*

ACOLYTE 1. When they burnt him that day . . . were you there,
did you see? When they flung his ashes into the Arno . . . all
his ashes . . . no relics, they said, no relics. And yet . . .
(*Opening a phial.*) . . . look, remember . . .

ACOLYTE 2. The grey eyes, the beak nose, that path on his skull . . .

ACOLYTE 1. . . . That mark of God. And that voice like thunder.

MICHELANGELO (*weakening*). I'll never forget that voice.

ACOLYTE 1 *and* 2 (*booming*). 'The black cross, the cross of God's wrath, the dagger of God above the earth . . . '

MICHELANGELO. Hush . . . please hush . . .

People are coming. MICHELANGELO *gives the* ACOLYTES *coins.*

God keep you. We'll talk again. Just leave me now . . .

MICHELANGELO *and the* ACOLYTES *exit in different directions.* SALAI *enters, leading* LEONARDO – *in reluctant mood.* VITO *watches from the shadows.* SALAI *beckons on one of* SODERINI's CLERKS. SALAI *gives him a purse. The* CLERK *exits.* LEONARDO *paces. Now the* CLERK *ushers on* SODERINI, *signing papers.*

SODERINI. But surely this isn't the way to. . . (*Looking up, he sees* LEONARDO.) Master.

LEONARDO. Excellency.

SODERINI. What an honour.

LEONARDO. Mine, Excellency, mine.

SALAI *signals to the* CLERK *who exits.*

SODERINI. You must grant us leave, we're on our way to . . .

LEONARDO. Excellency, I wonder if I may have a word, just a word . . . about this block of stone . . . ?

SODERINI *hesitates, then smiles. Blackout.*

Scene Five

Morning. VITO *asleep at the block.* OLD VITO *standing along-side.*

OLD VITO (*stroking the block*). And so the morning came when this giant was to set off on his giant journey. In truth, he would not shift from this spot for the next three years. And yet his journey . . . (*Whistles in awe.*) . . . it's the biggest journey marble can make. From stone to man. I wished him well that morning. Like we say in the quarries, I gave him my special fortune . . .

VITO *gets up and urinates against the block.*

(*Singing.*)
    This secret is told, to us only it's told
    Psssst, pssssst, pssssssst . . .

VITO (*singing*).
    . . . The poor man has nowt, not young nor old
    Pshhhh, pshhhhh, pshhhhhhh
    Yet he and the rich man, they both piss gold.

They laugh. The sculptor CONTUCCI *arrives. A* CLERK *gives him a white sash – the candidatus – which he pulls over his head.*

CONTUCCI. I'm not late, am I? (*Checks an official letter.*) No. Is there any word who it might be? (*Paces; to* VITO.) I hate these occasions . . . !

MICHELANGELO *arrives. As he's given the candidatus,* VITO *moves towards him, beaming.*

VITO. Ey . . . !

MICHELANGELO (*walking past*). Why do I see you every-where?

Now LEONARDO *arrives, with* SALAI *and* ENTOURAGE. *As* LEONARDO *is given the candidatus,* VITO *moves towards him, beaming.*

VITO. Ey . . . !

LEONARDO *smiles briefly, but avoids the embrace, patting scent onto his neck.*

CONTUCCI (*to* LEONARDO*; strained*). May fortune smile.

LEONARDO. And on you, good man, on you.

CONTUCCI. It'll be you. It's bound to be you. With your tremendous fame and . . .

LEONARDO. Fame. D'you know the tale of the great silver head? . . . It shone so sharply it threw no shadow of its own, and people could see it from far, far away, the brightest of bright moons, aglow by day as well as night . . . and then it came to pass that a man created a pair of black eyeglasses, and stole near . . . and what he saw shook him . . . for the great silver head was just a bare stone which a million snails had slimed and slick'd to glory.

CONTUCCI *smiles politely, paces on, and whispers to* VITO.

CONTUCCI. Did you hear that? It's true what people say of him . . . (*Gestures: 'Weird.'*) Sculpt? Can he sculpt? The giant horse of clay . . . what more need we say? He can paint, yes – when he's bothered to. The man's a dabbler, a daubler, a doodler, tries this, tries that. Those little books he carries round – showed me a page once, the design for some, oh I don't know, some nonsense – those little books are his masterpieces. It's a joke, his life, and the fuss people make of it, it's just a cartoon of a life, a sketch, a map. Where's the hard work, the application others put in, the hours of careful craft? Genius? My arse shows more genius as it fashions its morning stool. At least you get a result. Oh, a disgrace, a disgrace if he gets this!

CONTUCCI *paces away furiously. Meanwhile,* LEONARDO *spots* MICHELANGELO *and approaches.*

OLD VITO (*to audience, excitedly*). And then it happened. And I saw it – I saw it with these eyes – saw them meet. For the first time. And it was like, d'you know, the young challenger and the great champion. It was like, well, David and Goliath.

LEONARDO *reaches* MICHELANGELO *who bows his head.*

MICHELANGELO. All honour to you, Master. I am your humble . . .

LEONARDO. I know who you are.

MICHELANGELO. How?

LEONARDO. I had my people point you out.

MICHELANGELO. Where?

LEONARDO. When you viewed my cartoon at Santissima
Annunziata.

MICHELANGELO. Among those crowds . . . they pointed me
out?

LEONARDO *nods and waits. There is a return compliment to
be paid.*

Yes. It was good. The cartoon.

'Good' is inadequate. They both look up at the marble block.

LEONARDO. Well.

MICHELANGELO. Yes. (*Tightly.*) It'll be you. Everyone says
it'll be you.

LEONARDO. We shall see.

They part. A roll of drums and a trumpet call, and a BAND
leads on the two CLERKS, *followed by* SPINI *and*
PANDOLFINI, *followed by* MACHIAVELLI. *He carries a
scroll tied with a ribbon.* PANDOLFINI *steps up onto the
scaffolding table.*

PANDOLFINI. Could the candidates please assemble . . . (*As*
LEONARDO, MICHELANGELO *and* CONTUCCI *come
forward.*) . . . And now the honourable Commissioner from
the Opera del Duomo will say a few words. Thank you,
Commissioner.

PANDOLFINI steps off the scaffolding table and SPINI
steps on.

SPINI. Thank you, honoured Consul from the Arte della Lana. I
must, alas, begin proceedings with an apology. We hoped this
momentous commission would be presented by His Excellency
himself, the Gonfaloniere for Life, but, alas, unforeseen and
pressing matters of state have summoned him elsewhere . . .

SALAI (*whispers to* LEONARDO). He's not here. Something's wrong.

LEONARDO. Shush!

SPINI. . . . However, we are nevertheless extremely fortunate to have secured as our presenter no less a man than the honourable Secretary to the Second Chancery. Thank you, Secretary.

Applause as MACHIAVELLI *steps onto the scaffolding table.*

MACHIAVELLI. Thank you, Commissioner. And may I just add my own apologies to all assembled – I'm sorry that you were promised the Gonfaloniere for Life, and instead get a mere Secretary. (*After a ripple of laughter.*) My thanks also to you worthy candidates for participating in a competition which certainly sets our blood racing, but for you it is perhaps more a quickening of nerves. Personally speaking, it is truly an honour to be in the presence of . . . (*Specifically at* LEONARDO.) . . . the most divinely gifted of men . . .

CONTUCCI (*whispering*). A disgrace . . . !

MICHELANGELO. I agree . . . !

SPINI *and* PANDOLFINI. Shh!

MACHIAVELLI (*upping his gear*). Why David? Why David now? Why David on a colossal scale? Two vital reasons strike me. Firstly, it will be a Statement, a political statement if you will. After the alarming events of recent times, with the French arrival in upper Italy, it is to our surprise, and with our thanks on High, that we have not emerged as the conquered ones, but instead it is our neighbour, and so often our scourge, Milan. So in crude terms then – and do forgive this lapse in style – one could say that David is us, Florence, and that Goliath is them, Milan. Secondly, it will be a form of Magnificence, of Magnification. This Magnification will read: Florentine culture is back, Florentine culture is in the ascendancy again, Florentine culture was not completely consumed in the Bonfires of the Vanities, but it is rising from their ashes, phoenix-like, and once more it soars. Again you must forgive my crudity – oh I don't know what's wrong with me today – in referring to the Bonfires, I was committing a most grievous slander, for I am certain that no one assembled here ever attended the sermons of the Friar, the Mad Monk, 'God's Jaws', or ever followed his teachings . . .

Nervous laughter. MICHELANGELO *squirms.*

. . . Just as these days one is hard-pressed to find anyone in Florence who ever served the Medicis . . .

More nervous laughter. More squirming from
MICHELANGELO.

. . . We are now, thanks be on High, finally freed from the tyranny of either emperor dukes or mad monks – we are now properly a republic. The Republic of Florence. With David as an apt symbol. Young, brave, fearless, and ultimately victorious. Victorious over this Goliath and all others Goliaths, whether the French, or Rome, or Milan . . . well no, not Milan any more, poor old Milan.

Laughter and cheers.

CONTUCCI (*whispering*). I thought this statue was for the Duomo, for God, not Florence . . .

SPINI *and* PANDOLFINI. Shh!

MACHIAVELLI. And now it is my duty, my privilege, to announce the sculptor of this new great David . . . (*Opens the scroll and reads.*) 'Their Excellencies, the Consuls of the Arte della Lana meeting together with the Commissioners of the Opera del Duomo do, on a contract of hire and salary at six broad gold florins a month, appoint as sculptor of a certain marble figure called 'Il Gigante', the worthy Master . . . Buonarroti . . . citizen of Florence!'

The BAND *strikes up in celebration. Applause and cheers – while* SALAI *leads* LEONARDO's ENTOURAGE *in boos. After handing the scroll to a relieved* MICHELANGELO, MACHIAVELLI *exits, with* SPINI, PANDOLFINI, CLERKS, *and a bitter* CONTUCCI. *Meanwhile,* SALAI *draws* LEONARDO *aside.*

SALAI. The bitching, bastard, cunt-swilling swine!

LEONARDO (*shaken*). Maybe they wanted it to be on merit.

SALAI. Merit . . . ?! (*Indicating* MICHELANGELO.) You think she got it on merit? She got it because she's young and she's cheap!

LEONARDO. It doesn't matter, I'm not a sculptor, it – does – not – matter. Go home and pack our bags . . . we leave for Imola tonight.

SALAI (*frightened*). Imola. Ooh trallerina-lannila . . . !

LEONARDO. You like fighting? You'll get fighting.

SALAI. And Florence – what will she get? She didn't give you this . . . this giant . . . so now you go and serve her foe . . . a real giant . . . building his weapons, building his might, helping him to come marching this way. Mmm, this idea is starting to blood me up sweetly. Let's fan all the flames of hell onto this place.

LEONARDO (*exploding*). What . . . making or breaking . . . is that the choice? Oh, there's a thing – maker or breaker – which shall I be? Both devils, both hunting one another . . . every time you make art you risk spoiling it, every time you make war you risk losing it. Making or breaking . . . which, which, which? No, no – I'm just a man trying to earn a living . . . just trying to buy his freedom . . . !

He exits fast, followed by SALAI *and* ENTOURAGE. *At the same time, the* ACOLYTES *slip back into view, heading for* MICHELANGELO.

ACOLYTE 1 (*whispering to* ACOLYTE 2). Now we must have him, yes? Now he will be a great patron, yes?

ACOLYTE 2. Yes, yes, yes!

MICHELANGELO *tenses as he sees them.*

ACOLYTE 1. Brother, poor, snarled brother . . . calm.

ACOLYTE 2. Calm, calm.

ACOLYTE 1 *and* 2. Salutations on your triumph, salutations.

MICHELANGELO. What? But you . . .

ACOLYTE 1. Yes, but now let us not talk of equivocation.

ACOLYTE 2. Now let us talk of commodity.

ACOLYTE 1. Let there be a graven image, yes, but with a Blessing.

ACOLYTE 2. Let there be art, yes, but with Faith.

ACOLYTE 1 *and* 2. Art with Faith.

MICHELANGELO. But . . . that's what I already believe.

ACOLYTE 1. Good. And now take it from Christ Himself . . . (*Bringing out a phial of Savonarola's ashes.*) Do you believe that Christ spoke through his throat?

MICHELANGELO. Yes . . . I do.

ACOLYTE 1 *and* 2. Then let him bless this for you, brother.

MICHELANGELO. Please . . . yes.

The ACOLYTES *take pinches of ash from the phial, and sprinkle these on the marble block, praying feverishly.* MICHELANGELO *joins in.*

ALL. *Benedicite, omnia opera Domini, Domino, laudate et super-exaltate eum in saecula . . . Benedicite, montes et colles, Domino, benedicite, universa germinantia in terra, Domi . . . amen.*

MICHELANGELO *gives the* ACOLYTES *a purse of coins.*

MICHELANGELO (*emotional*). Thank you, oh thank you . . .

The ACOLYTES *exit as* WORKMEN *start securing the yard: closing the gate, blocking the duck-throughs. Lights change.*

Scene Six

The yard is sealed off – MICHELANGELO*'s private area now. He's alone with his giant block of marble, holding his breath. Opening his bag, he takes out his small clay maquette of David – with Goliath's severed head.* VITO *half-opens the wicket door in the gate, as nervous as a pet dog: 'Can I come in?'* MICHELAN-GELO *doesn't notice.* VITO *enters, doing a slow dance, stamping his feet, clicking his fingers.*

VITO (*singing*).
> In places high
> And in stone
> Good sweet things
> Can be grown.

MICHELANGELO. What's that?

VITO. From home. Our song for good beginnings. Master. When do I start?

MICHELANGELO. Look. There isn't anything for you to do. I'm not employing apprentices on this. Don't like them anyway. They're always . . . waiting to show off their gifts . . . waiting to steal yours.

VITO *stays put*. MICHELANGELO *strokes the block*.

It's strange to think . . . I wasn't even born when this arrived in Florence.

VITO. From Carrara.

MICHELANGELO. From Carrara.

VITO. The ancient Caesars fetched their marble from our quarries.

MICHELANGELO. I know.

VITO. My forebears quarried the blocks that built Rome. My people.

MICHELANGELO. Your people.

VITO. And my people . . . even maybe my pappa, my uncles . . . maybe they themselves cut him from the mountain. D'you know – I think they did. Aye, they did. Now I see him back on his feet – believe me – this is a Barattini job!

MICHELANGELO (*laughs*). There is a moment. When you first get a commission. It's hard to . . . you're filled with such rejoicing, such light. Light – that's the word – lightness . . . (*Crossing himself.*) It is Your lightness of course . . . it lifts me up, I ride on Your spirit, I rise to Your place. (*Pause. Turns to* VITO.) Only lasts a moment though. This lightness. And then the hitting starts. (*Touches the block.*) Hitting, hitting . . . hurting, hurting . . .

He stares at VITO. *A pulse of insects.*

I don't need an apprentice. But maybe a model.

VITO. A model?

MICHELANGELO. David. David himself. When I made this maquette I didn't use a model. Just needed to rough the shape. But now I'll need more detail. (*A beat.*) Could I ask you to stand. (VITO *stands.*) Could you take off your shirt. (VITO *takes off his shirt;* MICHELANGELO *assumes a steady analytical tone.*) You see. Your build. It's from your work. You're a mountaineer quarryman, am I right?

VITO. Aye, Master. Right on the edge of the cliffs.

MICHELANGELO. The eggshells.

VITO. Right there, Master.

MICHELANGELO. Yes. Holding yourself there, and swinging the mallets . . . there's a tension in your build, you see. The shape of your shoulders and hips. It might help . . . with his build . . . his tension. (*Begins to circle* VITO, *studying his body.*) You've not done this before?

VITO (*laughing*). Nay, Master . . .

MICHELANGELO (*points to bruises on* VITO's *shoulder*). What's this?

VITO. Oh. Aye. Beg pardon. I was in a masque, and things, they went, d'you know, hurlywind.

MICHELANGELO. A masque? What masque was this?

VITO. It was 'bout, uh . . . Ganymede.

MICHELANGELO. Ganymede? Well, you should not have been hurt. (*Fetches paper and chalk and starts sketching.*) The Rape of Ganymede should not be a violent tale. It should not be a lascivious tale – as sometimes twisted by certain men. Ganymede's soul is simply freed from its physical bondage and borne aloft to a sphere of Olympian bliss. (*Stops.*) Where was this masque? Who was doing this?

VITO. Him. With you today. D'you know – the other candidates? D'you know there was the skinny little one, the one we all knew wouldn't win. And then there was the rich one. Him. He made the masque.

A beat.

MICHELANGELO. You don't know who that is?

VITO. I think he's a, a, a rich man. With too much money and too much time. A maker of masques.

MICHELANGELO (*smiling grimly*). Well, yes, he is that in one form. But he is also an artist. He has done a mural in Milan which is . . . ! (*Speechless with admiration.*) He is probably the finest artist we have.

VITO. Holy Jesus! He said the name of his town, but . . . (*Whistles and stamps.*) Holy Virgin, hold me hard and fuck me blue . . . that was him? I spent a night with him.

MICHELANGELO. You spent a night with him . . . ?

VITO. Only this masque, d'you know.

MICHELANGELO. Listen. You must beware of that man. He is an unbeliever. Possibly unholy. Born as a bastard, y'know. The father taking gross pleasure in some farming bitch-girl . . . or witch-girl . . . no one knows for sure. There is talk of sorcery. He has been seen to write backwards. Or, in the marketplace, to buy caged birds, and send them back into the air. Why? Where is he directing them? But the worst of it is . . . and my tongue goes sour to even tell you this . . . he was once arrested on a charge of sodomy. Do you know what that word means?

VITO. Well . . . the Germans say it means 'Florentine'.

MICHELANGELO. Yes, I've heard that, and I don't think it's funny.

VITO. Beg pardon, Master.

MICHELANGELO. Now the Officers of the Night didn't have enough evidence against your maker of masques. So the case was dropped. But they never cleared him of the charge. Do you understand what I'm saying?

VITO. Aye, Master.

MICHELANGELO. Good. So be very, very careful of him. Now take off all your clothes.

VITO *strips naked*. MICHELANGELO *sketches*.

VITO. Master . . .

MICHELANGELO. Hush.

VITO. But Master . . .

MICHELANGELO. No, no – hush – now there must be only hush.

OLD VITO *appears*.

OLD VITO. So I hushed. And as he worked, looking at me with those, d'you know, pretend-dead eyes, I thought of, I don't know why, thought of home. Carrara. Car-ra-raaaaa. And of Maria. And Flavia. But I knew I could never tell of them. 'Course not. Tell of women? Naa. I could smell the air, boy, I could scent the way it was going. For him, for the other one too, when they looked at me, this . . . (*Indicates the genitals of young* VITO.) . . . this was the face they were seeing. And it is like a face, ey? C'mon, use your fancy . . . there's the hair, the nose, and those are like cheeks. For men, it's our other face. The face we hide away. (*A beat*.) D'you know . . . in my life I've sometimes thought . . . what if I was not a male?

MICHELANGELO (*to* VITO). Thank you. You may re-robe. (*As* VITO *dresses*.) Now what did you want to say?

VITO. Nay, it was nothing, Master. I was only going to ask – did you not want me to stand there with the sling?

Pause.

MICHELANGELO. You have a sling?

VITO. We all do, Master, in the mountains. You have to. Drive off wolves and lynxes, hunt rabbits and birds. Even to hunt honey you must hit the tree high.

MICHELANGELO. You have a sling . . . ?!

VITO. I call him the Scorpion, Master. You don't see him coming – phht! – you're dead – the Scorpion!

MICHELANGELO. And you have this . . . 'Scorpion' . . . with you?

VITO digs in his bag and brings out the Scorpion: two hemp straps with a leather pouch inbetween.

VITO. This strap is the handle . . . this one has the finger-loop. You load the stone – the scorpling. Then you must only do one turn. Or it can go wild, your aim. But do one clean turn, and you'll fly true. And as it flies, the scorpling will sing . . . (*Imitates the whistle of the stone.*)

MICHELANGELO. Show me again.

As VITO prepares to demonstrate another throw, he is possessed with fierce concentration.

Stay!

VITO freezes – though not in the exact pose of the finished statue.

Oh. It's before.

VITO. Master?

MICHELANGELO (*looking at his maquette*). It's not after, not with the severed head. It's before – before he's thrown it, before the stone is slang. Here is the moment. A moment all men know. Some fearsome battle. Be it in some kind of test . . . like winning a commission . . . or a sickness . . . or a temptation.

The pulse of insects grows.

There will be no payment. There will be food and shelter. In here. You will not be trained as an apprentice. You will never touch the stone.

VITO. Nay, but I'll tell you about him.

MICHELANGELO. You will sharpen chisels – I make my own – you will repair mallets, you will heat braziers, cook, and so on.

VITO. Aye, Master.

MICHELANGELO. And you will model. From time to time.

VITO. Aye, Master.

MICHELANGELO. Good.

VITO. Only one thing. There must be some money. Or else I go now.

MICHELANGELO. You sound like my father. It's all money, money, money. Where's the feeling?

VITO. Uh . . . you talking of me, Master? For there's plenty feeling. I want this work. But there must be something for me to take home – one day.

A beat.

MICHELANGELO. One florin. Every six months.

VITO. Six months?!

MICHELANGELO. This is going to take a long time.

A beat.

VITO. Done.

MICHELANGELO. Good.

VITO. Good. And . . . Master . . . will it look like me? The Giant. Will it be like statues of dukes and popes? Only this time it's Vito Barattini of Carrara.

MICHELANGELO. Of course not. God made you, and He made you perfect. But then He also made dozens like you, scores. I pass you in the street every day. You are simply a species of life. A herd of perfect men. Yet – ordinary, human, small. My task will be to awake the viewer to the blessedness of it again. I will attempt to achieve this partly by scale, and partly by invention. But I am not a copier. It will look nothing like you.

He starts to turn away. Then stops, and smiles at VITO.

I feel it again . . . that lightness. And it makes me think of David. Not the warrior . . . but the sweet Psalmist of Israel. Do you know of David's psalms?

VITO. Uh . . . probably should, Master, but probably don't.

MICHELANGELO. There's one . . . 'And he rode upon a cherub and did fly, and yea, he did fly upon the wings of the wind.' (*A beat*.) Come, there's much to be done.

VITO. Master . . . thank you.

VITO runs forward and kisses MICHELANGELO. MICHELANGELO *is flabbergasted. He goes over to the statue.* VITO *hugs himself, whistles, dances – then joins* MICHELANGELO. *They move the turntable round. As the lights start to change,* OLD VITO *comes forward.*

OLD VITO. It was a Monday . . . a fortnight afore Michaelmas . . . the thirteenth of September . . . in the second year of our new century. I don't hold dates. Don't use them. Use the seasons. But that date's carved in my head. He must've said it sometime that morning . . .

The scene changes to evening . . .

Scene Seven

. . . Low, yellow light filters into the yard. A ringing of insects and frogs. On the front of the marble block is now a huge dotted outline of David. Next to it, much smaller, a grid drawing. Strewn around are large sheets of paper with different parts of the figure. The lines on these are perforated, and MICHELANGELO *is using a pounce (a muslin bag of charcoal dust) to apply a tracing onto the last section of the giant body: the legs. The atmosphere is tense.* VITO *hunkers on the ground, watching. Meanwhile,* OLD VITO *continues.*

OLD VITO. . . . All day he worked on with spiked wheel and pounce, ghosting the figure onto the block. Just on the front. Which was other. Most carvers will go at a block any which ways. But he said he'd only go in on the front. Then he told me to hush. Then never said another word. Not till the lag end of that long day . . .

MICHELANGELO. No! Forcing my hand . . . ! Forcing his legs . . . !

He hits at the semi-carved section which dictates the position of David's legs. Growling, he climbs off the scaffold. Starts to pace. VITO keeps well back. MICHELANGELO picks up his drill, which resembles a miniature bow and arrow.

(*Muttering.*) Him with his sling, me with my bow, him with his sling, me with my bow, him with . . .

He throws the drill aside. Paces round and round, mumbling furiously. Then leans on his knees.

VITO (*quietly*). Shall you start now, Master?

MICHELANGELO. What? What are you talking about? Great God. You idiot, you fool, you child. 'Start' . . . ! (*Looks round wildly.*) What – now? The hitting, the hitting . . . the bloody hands, the hurting hands . . . now? No . . . not ready, not ready, not ready, not ready, not ready, not ready, not ready . . . !

Repeating this like a mantra, he collects his heaviest mallet, races up the scaffolding, and strikes the first blows. VITO has to look away. OLD VITO speaks to us.

OLD VITO. Those big punches. The mason punches. With the big mallet. You can be quite strong with them, d'you know. There's the quarry skin . . . lots of waste . . . lots to hit away. But you must still be careful. It's like everything with marble. This stuff is hard and soft, d'you see. One wrong blow and it's . . . ! (*Whistles.*) D'you see what I'm saying? You can't put it right, make it better. It's not paint. You can't cover over, start again . . .

VITO (*flinching as MICHELANGELO hammers away*). Hoh . . . !

OLD VITO. I'd never seen a man go at marble like that. Like he hated it. Yet also loved it. He had to have it, win it. See what I'm saying? He couldn't bear it.

VITO (*shying away from flying fragments*). Hoh . . . hoh . . . !

OLD VITO. It was like . . . the body in there . . . in the block . . . that beautiful boy . . . if he couldn't get to it soon . . . couldn't get it breathing . . . it was going to die.

MICHELANGELO *starts emitting hoarse, ugly grunts with each blow.*

That first day I got feared. Very feared. This fight was to the death. And I wasn't sure any more. Wasn't sure which one was David.

Lights fade as both VITO *and* OLD VITO *watch* MICHELANGELO *attack the block, using tools, fists, feet to hack at the top stone, desperate to reach the beautiful boy inside.*

End of Act One.

ACT TWO

Scene Eight

From the darkness – voices praying. Lights up. It's like an Arctic scene, with white marble waste everywhere. Praying are the Savonarola ACOLYTES *and* MICHELANGELO, *who murmurs along while carving. The statue can only be glimpsed through the scaffolding, but it's very advanced, and now has the power of the artist's unfinished works (like the Four Slaves), a naked, muscular man struggling to escape a prison of stone.* MICHELANGELO *is covered in the white mud of marble dust and sweat. The* ACOLYTES *– wearing only their white uniform with the red cross – walk in a continuous circle.* VITO, *also wearing a red cross, sits apart in his bed area. (*MICHELANGELO*'s bed area is at the other end of the yard, and there are also cooking and washing areas.)* OLD VITO *speaks to us.*

OLD VITO. I thought I'd lost my wits. I thought I had for sure. Week after week, month after month . . . (*Indicates the* ACOLYTES.) . . . '*Benedicite, omnia opera Domini, Domino*' . . . one and a half years of this! And they kept going on these, d'you know like, special fasts. Days and days when they could only have bread and wine. Aye – wine! Heads soon like their bladders, ey, dribble, dribble.

VITO (*as the* ACOLYTES *pass*). *Benedicite, omnia opera Domini* . . .

OLD VITO (*indicating* MICHELANGELO). And him . . . Some days he didn't eat – forgets to eat. Some days he didn't sleep – forgets to sleep. And as for washing – this he forgets every day. Phfff! So this is how it was on that morning . . . it was spring . . . outside the air was full of this soft white stuff . . . at home we call it proppo . . .

A knock on the door. The ACOLYTES *grab their robes and hide.*

MICHELANGELO. Yes . . . ?

The door opens. A little cloud of poplar-down blows in.
LEONARDO *is standing there, looking older, wearier.* SALAI
is behind him. MICHELANGELO *quickly pulls a rope,*
closing canvas curtains over David.

(*To* LEONARDO.) Oh. People said you'd come storming back
to Florence at the vanguard of a Borgia army.

LEONARDO. Me? Surely not.

MICHELANGELO. When did you . . . ?

LEONARDO. This very morning . . . and as soon as I reached the
city walls, a clerk from the Signoria was awaiting me with . . .
(*Waves a letter.*) It invites me to sit on the committee which
will decide where he . . . (*David.*) . . . will be placed.

MICHELANGELO. You. Him. (*Pause.*) But the placing is pre-
scribed. Isn't it? On the north buttress of the Duomo. Above
the Porta della Mandorla.

LEONARDO. Oh, have you not . . . ? Oh no, the commissioners
should give you this news . . . though no doubt you'll be
pleased to hear it . . . no, it is thought, by those who've had the
privilege of viewing the work in progress, that this giant David
should be placed on ground level where he can be fully
adored. May we enter?

MICHELANGELO *nods.* LEONARDO *and* SALAI *come in.*

(*To* VITO, *quietly.*) Good morning.

VITO. Good morning.

SALAI. Ah. We are back.

SALAI *finds the* ACOLYTES *and shrieks. The* ACOLYTES
flee.

LEONARDO. By blood, what was . . . ?

SALAI. Master, it . . . it was two of those whores from the old
days, I swear it was . . . those boy whores who turned into the
'Friar's Youth' . . .

MICHELANGELO. No – he's wrong. It was . . . well, I don't
know who it . . . people bring materials, food. (*To*
LEONARDO.) So yes – this letter of yours?

LEONARDO. Yes . . . this committee, it's made up of, oh, I can't recall . . .

SALAI. Only the most distinguished names in Florence. Filarate, the first Herald of the Signoria, the painters Granacci, Perugino, Tucci, and even Botticelli! The architects Pollaiuolo and the da Sangallo brothers, the master embroiderer Gallieno, the piper so-and-so and bi-bi and fu-fu . . . and then you, my Master, you!

LEONARDO. And then me, me . . . ah yes, this shall rank high among my achievements . . . 'A painter of portraits, an inventor of machines, and a sitter on committees.' (*To* MICHELANGELO.) At any rate, they say that . . . and I don't know why, but they say I'll be an influential voice. So I wonder if I may . . . ?

MICHELANGELO *reveals David.* LEONARDO *stares and stares.*

Yes . . . it's good.

MICHELANGELO *registers the word 'good'.*

This here . . . this is specially good . . . the sternum, the diaphragm . . . it's full of tension, full of breath . . . there's air in there, I can see it . . . you've put air into stone . . . he's holding his breath . . . and I'm holding mine. (*Pause.*) Oh, but I've only just realised . . . there's no head of Golia . . . ! This is before the battle.

MICHELANGELO (*smiling*). Why, would you have done him after? Like everyone else.

LEONARDO (*a beat, then:*). Never mind what I might have done . . . you're giving Florence a David before he fights the Philistine . . . and that's . . . extraordinary. I would only, and humbly, implore as you proceed to beware of excessive musculature . . . otherwise, instead of a human figure, one can end up with a sack of walnuts. (SALAI *sniggers*.) But no, at the moment it's . . . good.

VITO. And it's me.

LEONARDO *goes still. He stares at* VITO. *Then back at the statue.*

LEONARDO. Him. You.

SALAI. Is it? The Carra' man? Do we really have two Davids in this room? Oh yes . . . I can just see it now. (*To* VITO.) But oh darla – now we'll have to call you Mister Little Rock.

LEONARDO. Shush.

SALAI (*whispering to* VITO). And what a funny way you posed – with your face turned away, yet your little rock pointing straight at us.

LEONARDO. Peace!

MICHELANGELO. So – not up on the buttress? But it's . . . it's designed to be viewed from below.

LEONARDO. Ah well, alas.

MICHELANGELO. What then – in a niche?

LEONARDO (*checking the letter*). No . . . about half a dozen possible placings . . . but no mention of a niche.

MICHELANGELO. Oh . . . then I'll have to do the back.

LEONARDO (*peering round David*). Which might not be unin-teresting.

MICHELANGELO. Great God man, it's not a question of . . . ! It's time. Where's the time? Now I have double the work.

LEONARDO. Ah well. Now if this committee is expecting any guidance from me, may I . . . ? (*Shows his notebook.*)

MICHELANGELO (*a cold laugh*). Must say I'm surprised. You on a civic committee. Do they know where you've been? Who you've been working for?

LEONARDO. Oh yes – well, the Secretary was there too.

MICHELANGELO. The Secretary?

LEONARDO. At Imola, oh yes . . . he was sent there in his new office, as Foreign Emmissary, to parley with the Duke, to prevent him marching this way . . . and he ended up staying three months . . . winter months, icy winds on the plains, us holed up in the fortress . . . Oh thanks be for the Secretary! . . .

But MICHELANGELO *has gone back to work.* LEONARDO *looks for a clean place to sit.* VITO *wipes a bench.* SALAI *watches them intently.*

So how are you – Vito Barattini of Carrara – how are you?

VITO. Nay, I'm well. I've lost my wits in here, but that apart, I'm well.

LEONARDO. All right . . . here's one. Easy or hard?

VITO (*clapping his hands*). Hard.

LEONARDO. Creatures of different colours will be seen carrying men through the air to the destruction of their lives.

VITO. Birds! Eagles!

LEONARDO. No – soldiers on horseback. Easy really.

VITO *frowns.* LEONARDO *sketches David.*

VITO (*pointing to sketches on the other page*). What are these here?

LEONARDO. Hm? This is a sword-eating shield . . . this, a wall which can deflect all known weapons.

VITO. All known wea . . . ! You built these things?

LEONARDO (*laughing grimly*). No . . . I dream and dream, and the machinery crashes and crashes . . . (*Flicks through his book.*) Here's one-and-a-half years' work . . . one-and-a-half years of serving that foul, cunning man, that would-be Caesar . . . 'This weapon, how many will it slaughter?' . . . 'Oh, hundreds, Lordship' . . . 'And the mutilations, what will they be?' . . . 'Terrible decapitations, Lordship, slow dismemberings' . . . and so on, for one-and-a-half years . . . (*Watching* MICHELANGELO *carve.*) . . . while he made this. He's been with David, and I, truly, with the Philistines.

VITO. You seem . . . I dunno . . . changed.

LEONARDO. No, no, I'm just tired . . . it wastes you, this work. And nothing holds fast, except the mathematics . . . these little trails of numbers . . . these are my ropes threading through the dark, my ladders, my bridges . . . these are my little gods.

VITO. Maybe it's all . . . d'you know . . . simpler than you think.

LEONARDO (*laughing*). No, that is what I think . . . before Discovery, everything seems . . . dense and entangled and blocked . . . and you're just this curious creature, half scientist, half animal, just trying to sniff your way out of the dark . . . but after Discovery, yes, it's all much simpler.

VITO (*indicating David*). I mean, look now on his sling. The way we're making him throw it, the Master and me, it's going short, it's going hard, it's going to kill.

LEONARDO. It is, and more effectively than any of these . . . (*Indicating the war machines in his notebook.*)

VITO (*fetching his own sling*). But if he threw it more like this . . . it'd go lighter and further. And if he threw it really high . . . it'd glide . . . it'd . . .

LEONARDO. Fly.

VITO. Aye, it would.

LEONARDO. Aye. And if it was powered, and if it was winged . . . (*Jotting notes.*) Show me how you would throw it really high.

VITO (*whispering; indicating* MICHELANGELO). Not now. Later.

LEONARDO. I see, yes . . . later then.

Noticing them talking, MICHELANGELO *has deliberately moved down to work on David's pubic hair – using his drill (his 'bow') to define the curls.*

Ah sir, is that, pardon me, is that . . . private hair . . . I can see?

MICHELANGELO. It is.

LEONARDO. Well . . . this will again affect where the work is placed . . . I know of no public statue with private hair . . . not on this scale . . . not since antiquity.

MICHELANGELO. It was on the maquette. No one minded.

LEONARDO. But they might now it's the size of a rose bush.

VITO giggles. MICHELANGELO *throws a chisel at him.*

MICHELANGELO. Sharpen this! The point is not sharp! Why bother giving it back if it's not sharp?

VITO *sharpens the chisel*. LEONARDO *observes the situation*.

LEONARDO (*to* SALAI). Why don't you go home and open the shutters.

SALAI. Master . . . have you forgotten you have a noon sitting at the Piazza Santa Maria Novella? The silk merchant's house – his wife. And he's already tettish because you've been absent for so . . .

LEONARDO. And I'll be there, and I'll smile at him, and I'll promise him he'll have the finished work . . . next . . . whenever . . . so thank you, and go on.

SALAI. No, Master. I'm not sure you know the way. I'll wait and guide you. (*Privately.*) Oh be careful, pa-pa-paa. We've had a good, long stay at Imola . . .

LEONARDO. You'd call that a good stay?

SALAI. Us. We were good. You were talking to me again, listening to me again, prizing me again. And me . . . I've never loved you more.

LEONARDO *doesn't respond*. SALAI *makes a devil-sign to* VITO, *then marches to one side and plants himself there*. VITO *is scared*.

VITO (*whispers to* LEONARDO). Will you do me a favour?

LEONARDO. Only with pleasure.

VITO. Will you write for me? Home. I can't, y'see.

LEONARDO. That's all right, I'm an unlettered man too . . . as I told you once, we're both just country boys. Who d'you want to write to?

VITO. To Maria – who else? – my wife.

LEONARDO *splutters, while* MICHELANGELO *almost castrates David*.

And Flavia – our little girl.

LEONARDO *and* MICHELANGELO *both turn towards*
VITO.

LEONARDO. What . . . all this time away from them . . . and
you haven't . . . ?

VITO (*glancing at* SALAI, *whispering lower*). It's because of
him . . . the Little Devil . . . he said . . . but you'll not let him
massacre them, will you?

LEONARDO. Why would he massacre them?

VITO. Because they're there . . . my earthly kith 'n' kin . . . and
I'm here . . . in the clouds. (*Laughs.*) On my last night at home
. . . we were going to bless my journey here, me and Maria,
my journey to make us rich, bless it with a fuck. But we can't
– we're crying so much. So I get dressed and go to the house
of Sandro, the foreman. I say, Give me wisdom, old friend,
how do I say goodbye to my Maria? He says, You want
wisdom – here's wisdom. He brings out this bottle – it's
grappa, but, d'you know, of his own making. It's past midnight
when I go home. And there's Maria – eyes in the candlelight –
hot as hell. I say, Hail Maria, you're full of grace, I'm full of
grappa, let's just go to sleep. And d'you know what, Maria,
you're not going to mind me leaving in the morning. Sandro –
he gave me this wisdom. (*Laughs – then weeps.*) Oh I miss
them . . . ai! . . . it's like a hole in me.

LEONARDO. Look, no one will harm your family . . . (*Glares at*
SALAI, *then sits closer to* VITO *and takes out pen and paper.*)
What d'you want to say?

VITO. I love you.

LEONARDO *writes. Then awaits further dictation.*

I love you . . . I love you . . . I love you . . .

LEONARDO. Don't you want to say anything else?

VITO. What else is there? I love you . . . I love you . . . I love
you . . .

LEONARDO. Good, well, I think they'll get the point . . . here,
sign it.

He guides VITO*'s fingers on the paper.*

VITO. What have I written?

LEONARDO. The letter 'V'.

VITO (*keeping hold of his hand*). Thank you. Bless you . . .

MICHELANGELO (*wheeling round*). Look, I cannot work with this, all this . . . !

LEONARDO. No, no, of course not, forgive me . . .

MICHELANGELO. Have you seen what you need to see?

LEONARDO. Uhm . . .

SALAI. Yes, you have, Master, haven't you? – You absolutely have! – and now you need to be at the Piazza Santa . . .

SALAI *tries to usher him out, but* LEONARDO *is staring at* VITO.

LEONARDO. D'you remember a special place I once told you about?

VITO. The road, the lovely old road. Above the flying birds.

LEONARDO. Correct. (*Scooping up some poplar-down.*) And this is the time . . . the poppies opening in the olive groves . . . red flowers . . .

VITO. . . . Silver trees.

LEONARDO (*to* MICHELANGELO). Sir, before I can sit on this committee, I must make one more small journey. I've been away for so long, Salai and the others will have to open my house here, so . . . may I borrow your young Vito? Just for a short time. Servants can be wearisome, sometimes a break is advisable . . .

SALAI. Ah-la-la, excuse me . . . ! (*Takes* LEONARDO *to one side; whispers.*) What are you doing? You have a sitting at the silk merchant's . . .

LEONARDO. Tell him I'm ill, mad, dead, I don't care – I've had one-and-a-half years of foulness, now I want some fresh air . . .

SALAI. And him – you want him. Why? I can't believe this is happ . . . ! All the boys before – even me – it was always just look but no touch, eh? Now something's different. Ahh yes, ti-ti-tis. I can smell it, that brown sweat, the arse is in the air. But . . . why him?

LEONARDO. I don't know . . . and I hate that I don't know . . . don't look at me like that! . . . I don't know why.

SALAI. Well, I do. (*Indicating David and* VITO.) You couldn't have that David, so you'll try this one. Especially now you know it likes cunt. Here's one to win.

LEONARDO *shoves* SALAI *aside, and turns to* MICHELANGELO.

LEONARDO. So what do you say? I'll double his wages, half to him, half to you . . . and while we're away, think where you'd like him . . . (*David.*) . . . placed, and then in this committee, I'll do what I can.

Pause.

MICHELANGELO. Very well. Why not? Nothing for him to do at the moment anyway. (*To* VITO.) Is there?

VITO *shrugs, shakes his head, trying to contain his excitement.*

LEONARDO. Right then, sir, I'll borrow him, and you'll pardon me, I hope, for borrowing your time. (*Whispering to* VITO; *indicating the sling.*) Bring that with you.

VITO *fetches the sling.*

VITO (*to* MICHELANGELO). Take my leave, Master.

MICHELANGELO *says nothing.* LEONARDO *and* VITO *exit.* MICHELANGELO *and* SALAI *look at one another, both stunned. Then* SALAI *bursts into tears. He exits.* MICHELANGELO *sinks back against the scaffold.*

MICHELANGELO. Oh Jesu, you've caught me this time. You've caught me.

Lights change.

Scene Nine

*Night. It has been raining; water drips here and there, and there
are rolls of thunder. The yard is lit by braziers. Wearing an
improvised headpiece with a lit candle,* MICHELANGELO *is
feverishly carving the back of David. On the turntable, the statue
is facing front, with the curtains almost closed over it. The door
opens, and* MICHELANGELO's *father* LODOVICO *enters. His
manner is both grand and crushed. Pulling back his wet cloak, he
looks up at the statue – only David's genitals can be seen.*

LODOVICO. Oh God . . .

MICHELANGELO. Oh no . . .

> MICHELANGELO *closes the curtains fully.* LODOVICO
> *enters further, wrinkling his nose at the smell in the air.*

Ahh please – and who was it taught us that too much washing
is dangerous?

LODOVICO. Yes, yes, but so is too little.

MICHELANGELO. Are you well?

LODOVICO (*a martyr's tone*). Oh. Mainly. Yes.

MICHELANGELO. And the others?

LODOVICO. No. Yes. Well enough.

> *He dries his cloak against a brazier.* MICHELANGELO
> *fetches his purse.*

MICHELANGELO. May I . . . ?

LODOVICO. Oh. Well. Only if, y'know.

MICHELANGELO. Yes.

> *He doles out money.* LODOVICO *pockets it, almost resentfully.*

LODOVICO. It's only that, y'know, having to wash one's own
clothes, bake one's own bread . . .

MICHELANGELO (*wearily*). Yes, yes.

LODOVICO. It's just that, y'know . . .

MICHELANGELO. Yes.

LODOVICO. . . . With one's pedigree, one should be more settled by this stage of life . . .

MICHELANGELO. Mmn.

LODOVICO. . . . Maybe one should still wive again. Maybe. (*Crosses himself.*) Oh! I dreamed of her. Just last night. Do you?

MICHELANGELO. What?

LODOVICO. Dream of her.

MICHELANGELO. That is . . . a strange question. And you've asked it before. Do you know that you have?

LODOVICO. And shall again. Do you dream of her?

MICHELANGELO. What . . . ? How can I? I was tiny. How do you dream of someone you don't even remember?

LODOVICO. Because she . . . she was beautiful. Why is her beauty not burnt into your head? You – an artist – and you don't remember such beauty. An artist – and you don't dream of such beauty? My, my. You should be carving great stoneworks of her, not of . . . ! (*Crosses himself.*) Ah well. But then it's not in one's sphere, is it? What does one know? One knows nothing. Only that Man's creations cannot match God's. And so Art – or certainly stonework – seems to be separate from real beauty, like hers. (*Crossing himself.*) Ah me.

Moving away, he steps into a sticky puddle of rainwater and marble dust.

Tsk! This place . . . !

Paces uneasily. Then produces some documents.

And then there are these damned bills . . .

MICHELANGELO. Yes of course.

LODOVICO. Your brothers are such useless . . .

MICHELANGELO. Yes, yes, it's all right.

LODOVICO *accepts more money, resentfully again, and collects his cloak. In the distance, thunder rolls.*

LODOVICO. All the same. Everything is well?

MICHELANGELO. Yes.

LODOVICO. Good.

    LODOVICO *starts to go*.

MICHELANGELO. Don't.

LODOVICO. What?

MICHELANGELO. Could you be with . . . ? I'm . . .

    MICHELANGELO *cracks – weeping. He fights to control it, but exhaustion is ruling him.*

LODOVICO. Now, now . . . what's this?

MICHELANGELO. Nothing.

LODOVICO. Is it the work?

MICHELANGELO. No.

LODOVICO. Is it your health?

MICHELANGELO. No.

LODOVICO. Is it a woman?

MICHELANGELO (*starting to laugh*). Oh Father . . . !

LODOVICO. What?

MICHELANGELO. You've got five sons, four of them un-wived . . . and you ask . . . 'Is it a woman?'

LODOVICO. What does that mean?

MICHELANGELO. Nothing.

    He weeps again. LODOVICO *shifts in discomfort*.

LODOVICO. Who is she?

MICHELANGELO. She is . . . everything . . . she is there when you sleep, she is there when you wake . . . she is why you wake . . . she is why you work . . . she is the only thing . . . she is everything . . . she is nothing . . . she is.

Long pause.

MICHELANGELO *collects himself together. In the distance, thunder rolls.* LODOVICO *peers up at the night sky.*

LODOVICO. Unusual for May.

MICHELANGELO. It is.

LODOVICO. Please may it not augur badly. Please not one of those hailstorms . . .

MICHELANGELO. Your vegetable garden.

LODOVICO. Oh may God protect it. Without it, I don't know how . . .

MICHELANGELO *gives him more money.* LODOVICO *sighs heavily.*

MICHELANGELO. It is good to see you.

LODOVICO. Yes.

MICHELANGELO. And I shall see you next month.

LODOVICO. Oh. Yes. Maybe.

MICHELANGELO. God keep you, Father, go with care.

LODOVICO. Oh yes, yes . . .

LODOVICO *leaves.* MICHELANGELO *returns to work. The sound of thunder and dripping rainwater fades, and the lone singing voice takes over. In the shadows, a figure appears.* MICHELANGELO *doesn't turn, yet experiences what follows. The figure moves into the flamelight, which warms the heaps of marble waste into an image of a sunny hillside – with red poppies and silver olive trees. The figure is* VITO, *naked, walking lazily, half-joining the singing voice.* MICHELANGELO*'s back arches with the pleasure of this vision. But now there's the sound of great flapping wings, and the shadow of an enormous eagle falls across* VITO. *He looks up, half-frightened, half-thrilled, then is consumed by darkness.* MICHELANGELO *collects the big mason's mallet – and swings it through the shadows. Nothing. No contact. He tries again. This time there is contact – and yelps. The*

Savonarola ACOLYTES *rush from the shadows – where they've been sleeping – career round the yard, and exit.* MICHELANGELO *flicks his head – he can't tell if he's asleep or awake. Outside the lions roar. Lights change.*

Scene Ten

The roaring of one lion comes closer. Hot afternoon. MICHELANGELO *is polishing David's buttocks, using a pumice stone together with handfuls of straw and sand. He flicks his head – is he hallucinating again? – it really does sound like the lion is approaching. Along with a crowd and a civic band.* SPINI *and* PANDOLFINI *rush in.*

SPINI. Quick, quick, he's coming . . .

MICHELANGELO. What? Who?

PANDOLFINI. Oh Saint Giovanni – the air in here!

SPINI. Quick, quick, we must . . .

   SPINI *fans the yard by wafting the door to and fro, while* PANDOLFINI *grabs a broom and tries to sweep a path through the piles of marble waste.*

MICHELANGELO. Who's coming?

SPINI. Yes, he is, he is, quick . . .

PANDOLFINI. And a little help would be . . .

MICHELANGELO. Who is coming?

SPINI. The Gonfaloniere . . .

PANDOLFINI. He wants to see the Giant . . .

MICHELANGELO. No . . . ! (*Shutting the door.*) It's not ready for . . . ! I don't like people . . . seeing, staring, judging . . . when it's not . . .

SPINI. Too late, too late – they're here!

MICHELANGELO *closes the curtains over David*. SPINI
opens the door. A GUARD OF HONOUR *enter. Then*
MACHIAVELLI, *then* SODERINI. SPINI *and* PANDOLFINI
take their place to one side. We hear a LION-HANDLER
resting the beast. The BAND *and* ONLOOKERS *peer in*
through the doorway.

MICHELANGELO (*bowing reluctantly*). Excellency . . .
Secretary . . .

SODERINI. Oh no, no, Master, please, it is us who should be
paying respects, for you are doing Florence a great service.

MACHIAVELLI. Worthy Master, do forgive us for coming upon
you so unexpectedly, but we were on procession to the Palazzo
Vecchio, for a meeting with the Signoria – when His Excellency
suddenly stopped, lost in thought – perhaps picturing the hours
of tedium ahead . . .

SODERINI. Oh no. Well, yes.

Everyone laughs.

Especially the debate on Pisa and why we seem unable to
retake the damned place again.

MACHIAVELLI. Indeed. And then he said, 'I wonder how the
Giant is coming along?' So we decided to find out.

SODERINI (*pretending to look round*). Now let's see . . . where
is he?

Laughter. MICHELANGELO *shifts uneasily.*

MACHIAVELLI. Worthy Master – may we? Please.

MICHELANGELO *opens the curtains. Everyone gazes up at*
David. MACHIAVELLI *leads a round of applause.*
MICHELANGELO *hates this.*

We are truly in the presence of a giant . . . (*To* MICHELAN-
GELO.) . . . And the giant is you.

SODERINI. Oh truly it is!

PANDOLFINI. But where's the head? (*Everyone is mystified.*)
The Philistine's head. Goliath's . . .

MACHIAVELLI. Yes, that is the masterstroke – it's before the combat!

Everyone echoes, 'Before the combat!' Another round of applause.

PANDOLFINI (*muttering*). But it's my favourite bit, the head.

SPINI. Shh.

SODERINI (*to* MICHELANGELO). Tell me – how do you actually do it?

MICHELANGELO. Well, I . . .

He feebly mimes a mallet and chisel. MACHIAVELLI *steps in:*

MACHIAVELLI. I'm especially intrigued by how you judge where to stop. That solid block which we all saw – you enter it, as it were, and keep going, but how do you know when you're there? At his elbow or knee . . .

SODERINI. Or his . . .

MACHIAVELLI. Well no, presumably that comes forward to meet the Master.

Laughter. MICHELANGELO *suffers. Then he demonstrates, placing a small upright box over a wax maquette.*

MICHELANGELO. The box is the original block . . . the figure is what I'm seeking to release . . . I put these in . . . (*Inserts rods through perforations in the box.*) I paint what's left sticking out black . . . I paint what's inside white . . . now I have pointing marks and measurements . . . I multiply these . . . it's very simple really.

SODERINI. Oh no, too modest.

MICHELANGELO. Excellency, I can take no credit. Pointing is a technique handed down from the Greeks, the Romans.

MACHIAVELLI. But brought to perfection by our own Florentine giant. (*He leads another round of applause.*)

SODERINI. And tell me, which of these implements is your favourite?

MICHELANGELO (*with an inward sigh*). The gradino,
Excellency, the claw chisel. You can virtually crosshatch . . .
like with pen or chalk . . .

There's a commotion outside – the lion growling, the
ONLOOKERS *excited.* LEONARDO *and* VITO *push through*
the group at the door.

VITO. Sacred Mary, there's a ramping lion out here . . . !

MACHIAVELLI (*to* LEONARDO). Ah – my friend.

LEONARDO. Honoured Secretary.

MACHIAVELLI. Ah no, please. And in truth, I have a new title.
As do you – 'Survivor'. (*Announcing to the others.*) This
fellow and I, we survived the fortress at Imola!

Laughter. LEONARDO *glances at* MACHIAVELLI *uneasily.*
Meanwhile, MICHELANGELO *is staring at* VITO *in horror.*
LEONARDO *has dressed him in finery, curled his hair,*
painted his face.

(*To* LEONARDO.) Do you know our Gonfaloniere, The Most
Excellent Piero Soderini?

SODERINI. He does, we do. Master.

LEONARDO. Excellency.

SODERINI (*privately; indicating David*). Our regrets this
couldn't come your way.

LEONARDO. Thank you, Excellency, but that's in the past.

SODERINI (*publicly; to* LEONARDO *and* MACHIAVELLI).
Well . . . he's spared us his warmongering, the Duke at Imola, so
clearly your suffering was well spent. Our thanks to you both.

Puzzled, LEONARDO *glances at* MACHIAVELLI.
MACHIAVELLI *signals: 'Tell you later.'*

LEONARDO (*nudging* VITO *forward*). Excellency, may I
introduce . . .

MICHELANGELO (*furious*). Excellency, this is one of my junior
servants. He's had some time off work. And some ideas above
his station. (*To* VITO.) Go and change.

LEONARDO (*as* VITO *starts to retreat*). He is also, Excellency –
I think the Master omitted to mention this – he is also the
model for David.

SODERINI (*looking from* VITO *to* David). Are you truly?

VITO (*starting to tear off his clothes*). D'you want me to show
you?

LEONARDO. No!

Laughter. MICHELANGELO *fumes.* VITO *goes behind the
statue.*

SODERINI (*to* MICHELANGELO). So you were saying . . .
your 'claw chisel'. And these . . . ?

MICHELANGELO *is forced to take* SODERINI *on a tour of
the yard.*

MACHIAVELLI (*to* LEONARDO). Look here, you should know,
in my dispatches to the Signoria from Imola, I thought it best
to . . . freely interpret your work there. I may not have actually
said 'military engineer', I may have said . . . 'court painter' or
'master of masques' . . . I may even have said you were our
spy there.

LEONARDO (*amused*). Thank you.

MACHIAVELLI. No, no, dear me, we both understand the world.
Necessity. That word, so Florentine – it rules the arts as it does
government. We do what we must do. Sometimes there is
space for moral law, sometimes not. Oh, it is good to see you
again!

LEONARDO. And you, and you. (*Offering a phial of scent.*)

MACHIAVELLI. Ah, you still have these – thanks be. (*Indicating
the smell in the yard.*) Yes, this is a bit . . . isn't it? (*They
laugh.*) Now look, you must help me too.

LEONARDO. Only with pleasure.

MACHIAVELLI. I've been accused. One of those anonymous
notes to the Officers of the Night. The charge is serious. It's of
sodomy.

LEONARDO *goes still.*

Mine is with a woman, of course.

LEONARDO. Of course.

MACHIAVELLI. The tight arse – best grip of all, hm?

LEONARDO (*uneasy*). I don't indulge, my friend, not any more.

MACHIAVELLI. No, no, of course you don't . . . (*Winks, glancing at* VITO *who has reappeared.*) . . . At any rate, how did you overcome it, your trouble?

LEONARDO. Surely . . . you don't need me to advise you on this . . . you must have so many . . .

MACHIAVELLI (*with a dangerous smile*). But I want you to tell me. A little test of trust.

LEONARDO. Look . . . the case against me, it simply . . . fell away.

MACHIAVELLI. Fell away?

LEONARDO. There was talk that we were aided by . . . well, one of the men accused with me was related to the Medicis . . .

MACHIAVELLI. Oh I see.

LEONARDO *glances at* SODERINI, *who is climbing onto the scaffolding.*

LEONARDO. I'm sure you won't have trouble – seeking similar aid.

MACHIAVELLI. Oh no, no, of course Soderini will help. Soderini had better. He was accused himself, a few years ago, a sodomy charge also, not sure what gender. And ever since then, whenever he tries to interfere with the smooth running of government, we simply say – Sod Soderini. (*They laugh. Pause.*) Up the arse, up the quim, twixt dugs or ballocks, sucking his nature, tonguing hers, wielding whips and nooses, coupling with cadavers or infants or beasts of the field, it's all allowed, my good friend – so long as we conform, so long as we show the world what we are not. (*Brief pause.*) But the sin itself – this is essential. If we don't visit the shadows – y'know, just at the mouth of the cave, where it's still cool and enticing – if we don't do this, we are incomplete as human creatures.

LEONARDO. Ah that cave, those shadows . . . (*Catches himself.*) Oh, is it not absurd that you – even you – should be accused? And with a woman! Is this the new free Florence of ours? What free place has Officers of the Night?

MACHIAVELLI. Well, freedom is a wild animal – it must be tamed before you ride it. We can't license the cave – not just yet. But when we do, the Officers of the Night will become the Officers of the Cave, and they'll charge you to enter, and there'll be stalls and souvenirs, and suddenly it won't be half as exciting. But, yes, it will represent truer freedom. In the meantime, let Florence be . . . Florence.

SODERINI *is halfway up the scaffolding with* MICHELAN-GELO.

SODERINI. . . . You don't think the nose is perhaps a little big? (*Addressing everyone.*) One was just wondering whether the nose isn't a little big?

Everyone starts muttering – 'The nose . . . is it a little big?' MICHELANGELO *grabs some tools and, unseen from below, he pretends to chip at David's nose, while scooping up some marble dust and spilling it over* SODERINI.

MICHELANGELO. Oh Excellency, pray mercy . . .

SODERINI. No, no, please . . . Oh, but that's much better. (*To everyone.*) Isn't that better?

Everyone murmurs, 'Much better, much better', and applauds.

MACHIAVELLI (*to* LEONARDO). Right, now look, I have two commissions for you.

LEONARDO. Two? Excellent. Tell me.

MACHIAVELLI. Both with the flavour of War, I'm afraid, but that is my new office – as Secretary of it.

LEONARDO. You know my feelings, my friend – war is a union of madness and . . .

LEONARDO *and* MACHIAVELLI. . . . Necessity!

MACHIAVELLI. War is also the politician's favourite sport. Which is why we end up in Hell. Or at any rate, the best of us do. Now – which d'you want to hear first? Easy or hard?

LEONARDO (*laughing*). Oh easy . . . please.

MACHIAVELLI. A fresco. In the council hall of the Palazzo Vecchio. There are two spacious stretches of wall and I want two 'Battles' on it. Will you do one of them? At fifteen florins a month.

LEONARDO. Absolutely.

MACHIAVELLI. Good. Now . . .

LEONARDO. The hard one.

MACHIAVELLI. Yes. You as military engineer again – but for us this time, please. I'm afraid it's Pisa.

LEONARDO (*groaning*). Ohhh.

MACHIAVELLI. Yes, yes, that silly little republic – ever since the French left – yes, they've become very wearisome – so yes, we must make them ours again.

LEONARDO. Right, well, it's simple actually.

MACHIAVELLI *laughs*.

No, no – it is. We move the river.

MACHIAVELLI. What?

LEONARDO (*sketching in marble dust on the ground*). The Arno, we move it . . . for while Pisa has its port here, at the mouth of it, they have access to everything, and in every direction . . . so we move it, the Arno . . . probably here, at Livorno, the fenny marshland, the Stagno . . . we divert this water here by weirs . . . create a massive ditch here, fork it into two canals . . . no, this'll take men too long . . . so we create a digger machine here . . . and meanwhile in Pisa itself, we cut off their drinking water, their route to the sea . . . we leave them, in every sense, high and dry.

MACHIAVELLI. This is achievable . . . ?!

LEONARDO. Absolutely, make out a contract and I'll start immediately . . . I'll need an advance fee though . . . at present I'm a little . . .

MACHIAVELLI. Yes, yes, of course.

(*Calling to* SODERINI.) Excellency! It's solved, Excellency, the matter we were discussing.

SODERINI. Ehrm . . . ?

MACHIAVELLI. The matter of Pisa, Excellency.

SODERINI (*groaning*). Ohhh.

MACHIAVELLI. I know, Excellency, but it's solved – we simply move the Arno.

SODERINI. Move the Arno?

MACHIAVELLI. That's right, Excellency, this man here, this gifted man, he already has draft plans, we'll show you later, but the fact of it is – we move the river!

SODERINI. We move the river!

Everyone cheers, 'We move the river!' LEONARDO *beams while* MICHELANGELO *fumes – how in the presence of the Giant has he been upstaged?*

(*To* MICHELANGELO.) Thank you, worthy Master, it has indeed been a privilege to view your giant David.

PANDOLFINI (*muttering*). How would one even know it's David – without the head?

SPINI. Shh.

SODERINI (*to* MICHELANGELO). Now when can we have him?

MICHELANGELO. When he's finished.

SODERINI. Finished? But . . . good as. Yes?

MICHELANGELO. No . . . !

Silence. SODERINI *frowns.* MACHIAVELLI *steps foward.*

MACHIAVELLI. Excellency, to my eye it certainly looks . . . close to being finished . . . but artists see differently, I suspect. (*To* LEONARDO.) Am I right?

LEONARDO. In matters of Art, Excellency, we seek perfection – that is our scourge.

SODERINI. Oh really? In matters of State we never bother, and
that, I suppose, is ours.

Everyone laughs – and prepares to leave.

(*To* MICHELANGELO.) Ah well . . . your perfection then,
Master . . . but please . . . sooner rather than later?

MICHELANGELO. I'll try, Excellency – and just one final
matter – the nakedness – it is acceptable?

SODERINI. The nakedness. (*To* MACHIAVELLI.) Ehrm . . . ?

MACHIAVELLI. Oh . . . well, we must take advice, Excellency
. . . I've certainly never seen this . . . hair . . . on a civic
statue. And on such a scale. But we'll take advice, I'm sure
some solution can be found.

MICHELANGELO. Solution?

MACHIAVELLI. Some suitable adornment, a fig leaf or garland . . .

MICHELANGELO. No!

His explosion startles the yard. Then MACHIAVELLI *goes to
work.*

MACHIAVELLI. Of course not, worthy Master, nothing will be
done without your consent. You are, as earlier acknowledged,
the true giant here. (*Leads applause, then:*) Just one query . . .
unless my readings of the Scriptures are very slack, and God
forgive me they could be . . . was not David a Hebrew?

MICHELANGELO. Of course he was, Secretary.

MACHIAVELLI. It's only that you seem to have skipped the
circumcision.

*Everyone murmurs, 'Circumcision . . . he's skipped the circum-
cision.'* MICHELANGELO *is mortified. Then grabs mallet
and chisel, and aims at David's penis.*

LEONARDO. No!

EVERYONE. No!!

MACHIAVELLI. No, Master, leave it please. Leave him as one
of us.

Everyone laughs and cheers, 'One of us!'

Though perhaps, for reasons of accuracy, both historical and tribal, a fig leaf might be advisable?

More laughter. MICHELANGELO *tries to join in, but he's been trumped.* MACHIAVELLI *gives a signal, and the* BAND *starts playing. The lion roars.* MICHELANGELO *is forced to usher out* SODERINI, MACHIAVELLI *and their party, leaving* LEONARDO *and* VITO *alone.* VITO *gazes up at the statue, and talks to it.*

VITO. Are you not strange? I've looked on you day after day, month after month, I've watched you change and grow. But now . . . and it's only a thin time away . . . now I see you like a thing at first light. That clear. And you're no longer mine.

LEONARDO. Yours?

VITO. I'm talking of the stone I know at home. That massy stuff. Far as I know, it can't feel, can't think. But look at him now. Because when I do, d'y'know, it's like I'm drunk or sick or mad or all. But happy. Maybe this is like flying. It's . . . it's . . . (*Clicks, stamps, laughs.*) . . . what is it? Give me the word.

LEONARDO. Art.

VITO. Art. Nay, I don't know art. All I know is . . .

LEONARDO. Climbing and working, yes, eating and sleeping and fucking, yes . . . and now art too . . . and that's all right . . . he's changed and you've changed.

VITO. Me? Nay, nay. But all the same . . .

As he walks round the statue, MICHELANGELO *returns – unnoticed.*

. . . I mean, look now on the arse. Since we saw him last.

LEONARDO (*moving round to view David's rear*). Oh . . . yes.

MICHELANGELO. You must not do this! You two. You must not bring him . . . (*David.*) . . . down, down. You are those who cannot contemplate beauty unless it be lewd and shameful. In *The Inferno*, the Master writes of a filthy scrum of men . . .

'Those violent against God, Nature and Art, forced to walk in an endless ring, on a burning desert, in the Seventh Circle of Hell.'

LEONARDO (*coldly*). We were not, please be clear, admiring the arse. We were admiring your skill in portraying the arse. Personally speaking, I happen to think the arse a repellent organ. It shits, it farts, it stinks, it is a living sewer. I have anatomised it.

MICHELANGELO. So have I.

LEONARDO. Good, so then you'll know in all the body there is no more sickening pocket of flesh. Completely repellent. And like all the sexing organs, it . . .

VITO (*laughing roughly*). Sexing organs – the arse?

LEONARDO *goes silent. A beat.*

LEONARDO (*to* VITO). Thank you for our time together . . . thank you.

VITO. Nay . . . thank you.

VITO *embraces* LEONARDO. MICHELANGELO *watches.* LEONARDO *exits.* MICHELANGELO *grabs* VITO, *smudging the face paint, messing the curls in his hair.* VITO *fights back.*

Don't do that! If this sets you wrong . . . (*His face and hair.*) . . . 's a fair thing. But . . . hoh! I am Vito Barattini of Carrara. And nobody does that to me!

They glare at one another. MICHELANGELO *strides back to work.* VITO *goes to a pail of water and washes his face and hair.* OLD VITO *comes forward, observing the two of them.* MICHELANGELO *slams down his tools.*

MICHELANGELO. No . . . ! I charge you – the truth – what did you do at that place of his?

VITO. Nay nothing, Master. Just sat on the hilltop, just looked at the land, he pointed out things, I pointed out things, we're both just country boys.

MICHELANGELO. Hh! Were you not bored?

VITO. Aye, Master, very bored.

OLD VITO. Nay. Happy! Oh God the Father – so happy! On that hilltop. With the greatest man in Italy. And all he wanted was to be with me. And his head, y'know, that beautiful head. That beautiful head and that beautiful hill – we saw everything, knew everything.

MICHELANGELO. And at night?

VITO. At night I slept, Master.

MICHELANGELO. Did he . . . come to your bed?

VITO. Tell the truth, Master, I thought he might. He was going to try this, try that – a touch, a kiss. And I was going to try this, try that – like a fist in the nose . . .

OLD VITO. . . . Or a kiss back. Or naming my fee. (*Laughs*.) Don't tell Maria, ey? – To this day, she'd still kill me!

VITO. But nay, he didn't ever come.

OLD VITO. Yet why not? What was the matter with him? Or me? (*Looks at his younger self*.) Was I not beautiful?

MICHELANGELO. So – nothing happened?

VITO. Nothing, Master.

OLD VITO. Aye nay. Something did happen. I can confess it now . . . I'm too doddered to blush any more. Something happened. In me. New feelings. I . . . I couldn't stop watching him, following his trail, smelling his scent. And then I thought – oh no, it's got me. My arse may be safe, but my heart is Florentined. (*Laughs*.) Don't tell Maria, ey?

MICHELANGELO (*hurling a mallet at* VITO). I don't believe a word!

VITO (*dodging away*). Master . . .

MICHELANGELO. Oh hush man, hush!

VITO *curls up in a corner, wretched. He takes a red poppy from his pocket.* OLD VITO *looks at him tenderly.*

OLD VITO. And now I was in a right rough hurlwind. Sweet with men? Sweet with art? I wasn't me any more.

Lights change.

Scene Eleven

*Night. Late. Sweltering. The Sirocco is blowing, rattling the
timber walls, and making the lions roar more than ever.*
MICHELANGELO *is out of sight, carving David's back.* VITO *is
slumped on a stool, half-asleep.* OLD VITO *turns to us.*

OLD VITO. It was the heart of summer when now it happened. A
big old sweat wind was sharking through the city, and everything was up and angry. And he'd put us on one of those fasts
– ever since I got back – nothing but bread and wine . . .

MICHELANGELO *cries out. He comes into view clutching
his wrist – it's bleeding. He's working stripped to the waist, his
top half coated in white marble mud.*

MICHELANGELO (*clicking his fingers at* VITO). Hey! . . . hey!
Where are those clouts? A chip got me again.

VITO. Hhh . . . ? (*Looking at the wound.*) Master, that's deep.

MICHELANGELO. Give me those clouts.

VITO. Master, we must wash it . . .

MICHELANGELO. Hush, man – do as told.

Walking unsteadily, VITO *collects strips of cloth – and a bowl
of water.*

Did I ask for that?

VITO. Nay, Master, but we must wash it, Master.

MICHELANGELO. 'Must wash it.' People wash too much.

VITO. Aye, Master . . . (*As he washes and bandages the wound,
his actions are clumsy.*) Pardon, Master . . . 'S just today,
Master . . . can't do nothing . . . don't know nothing . . . I'm
only just born.

MICHELANGELO. What's the matter with you?

VITO. Just so hungry, Master.

MICHELANGELO. Hungry? Have you not had today's ration?

VITO. I have, Master . . . and tha's the problem, Master.

MICHELANGELO. It will purify us. It is Christ's body, Christ's blood coming into us. His pure body, pure blood. Pureness coming into you – for once.

VITO (*wearily*). Aye, Master.

The wind rattles the walls. They look at one another strangely, both drunk.

MICHELANGELO. Have I spoilt it?

VITO. Master?

MICHELANGELO (*nodding towards David*). Go and look. Under the left shoulder blade. The skin next to the strap. Have I spoilt it?

VITO goes to look. MICHELANGELO waits tensely. Silence.

Is it spoilt?

VITO (*returning*). Nay, Master.

MICHELANGELO (*crossing himself*). Thanks be. Can always tell when you're going to spoil it. Worked too long. Can't see it any more. Well . . . you can see it, but . . . don't know what it is. Not a patch of skin. Don't even know what skin is. Just a patch of stone. Stone, not skin. How did you think stone could be skin? And then you spoil it. You almost want to. Well . . . God's been merciful this time. (*As VITO starts to walk away.*) No – wait – bring the wine.

VITO fetches wine; MICHELANGELO drinks deeply.

Now . . . go over there. No. Stay. Turn round. Come here. Stay. Go there . . .

VITO. Ey . . . what's going on, Mas . . . ?

MICHELANGELO. 'Master' – that's what's going on! 'Master' – hear the word – 'Master.' Now – run! Stay – and – turn! Go there!

VITO (*stumbling drunkenly*). Jesu . . . I'm only just born . . .

MICHELANGELO. Oh – well then – lie down. Roll over. Turn. No – just your head – turn it away . . . (*Hesitates.*) Stand up. Go to hell! This wind . . . 's straight from Satan's sea . . .

(*Clicking his fingers*.) Right – my drawing things!

VITO *fetches paper, a board, chalk.*

Right. Disrobe.

VITO. Master?

MICHELANGELO. You're paid to model. So – model.

VITO. As David, Master?

MICHELANGELO. Who else? You want to try Goliath?

VITO. But . . . (*Looks up at the statue*.) . . . is it not a bit late, Master?

MICHELANGELO. Hush, man – what do you know? It's skin I need to see again. Not stone – skin. (*Clicking fingers*.) C'mon, c'mon!

VITO *strips, his balance wavering. He tries to adopt the David pose, but can't quite work out the contrapposto stance, or which arm goes where.*

Sing. Sing to me. That song of David's . . .

VITO (*singing*).
      And he rode upon a cherub and did fly
      Yea, he did fly upon the wings of the wind . . .

As VITO *continues quietly,* MICHELANGELO *sketches, head bowed.*

MICHELANGELO. You know, I . . . while you were away . . . I wasn't well. Kept seeing things. Your face. Carved every-where. Street cobbles, bread, smoke . . . your face everywhere. D'you understand?

VITO (*swaying about*). Huhh?

MICHELANGELO. Yes . . . 'huhh'! Yes . . . you're so far from being 'only just born'. You! You've been in this world a thousand other times.

VITO. Master, pardon, but I must . . . (*Sits on a stool*.) Master, I don't think I know what you're talking abou . . .

MICHELANGELO. Oh do you not now, do you not?! (*Pause*.)

Ohh. He must be a cripple, eh? Trying to carry away my dark. Trying to carry near your light. Must be a cripple by now. Eh?

VITO. Who must, Master?

MICHELANGELO. Love.

VITO. Love . . . ?

MICHELANGELO (*head buried*). And what d'you say to that now?

VITO *mumbles something, slips off the stool, and passes out.* MICHELANGELO *stares in disbelief. Then starts laughing.*

And I've only waited two years to tell you.

(*He stumbles towards* VITO, *muttering.*) Not ready, not ready, not ready . . .

A knock on the door. Before MICHELANGELO *can react, it opens.* LEONARDO *is there. He carries a large satchel. Behind him lurks* SALAI. *From where they're standing, they can't see* VITO *on the floor.*

LEONARDO. Forgive us . . . we've been working late, and we were passing. Look . . . I've been thinking . . . it's the boy . . . we must send him back to Carrara . . . back to his wife and daughter . . . Salai will arrange everything.

MICHELANGELO. Right. Only one obstacle I can see. You've been thinking, you've made a plan . . . but he's my servant.

LEONARDO. Yes, and I ask your pardon and I offer you payment. (*As he moves forward, he sees* VITO.) What have you done to him . . . ?

MICHELANGELO. No, no – what have you? (*Covering* VITO *with a drape.*) Ever since he came back from that place of yours, he's been . . . weak, unfit . . . a moment ago he fainted. What did you do to him? People say you're an alchemist.

LEONARDO. Though you of course know that's nonsense.

MICHELANGELO. I don't. I know that you're not a believer.

LEONARDO. Except in Man.

MICHELANGELO. Don't you mean boys?

LEONARDO. No, I don't – I mean you, me, him, everyone – Man – we are the miracle, the light, the life. It is us.

MICHELANGELO (*shudders and crosses himself*). What did you do to him in that place?

LEONARDO. Nothing. I sketched him, watched him. There were times when . . . on the hillside . . . he loves sunlight . . . he would disrobe and walk round basking . . . rejoicing in the sun . . . my sun, my air, my birthplace . . . and here was this boy walking naked . . . through the field poppies, and with the shade of the olive trees, the shade and the sun, these going over him like hands . . . unforgettable.

MICHELANGELO. And, what . . . ? Great God, man, you're asking me to believe no sin occurred?

LEONARDO. I don't care what you believe, it's the truth.

SALAI. The truth? 'He loves sunlight . . . he'd disrobe, walk round naked'?! (*Laughs, indicating* VITO.) No, the truth is, tu-tu, za-za, she just wanted it, she's just a little bitch-boy who's hungry on heat. And yet nothing happened. Why? Because she's . . . well, it's what everyone always says about you, isn't it? She's just another job you can't finish.

LEONARDO. Wait outside.

SALAI. But I tell the true truth. Isn't it what you love in me?

LEONARDO *slaps him hard*. SALAI *slinks away, and exits*.

MICHELANGELO. What . . . nothing happened?

LEONARDO (*exploding*). Look, try and . . . look, I had a fright once, a bad fright! I was only twenty-four, and all my dreams, my plans, my flesh itself, could all have gone up in smoke, and I mean smoke, I mean the stake. I took a vow of purity then – it wasn't easy, it wasn't easy – but now I hold it dearer than any priest . . . theirs bring them nearer to God they say, mine to a million other wonders. When you take all this – (*Grasping his own crotch.*) all this blood and seed and force, and you lift it into your skull, and oh here's a hard one now – now fuck, now fuck – now make your creations, your future! (*Pause.*) We cannot have greater lordship than over ourselves.

MICHELANGELO. Yes. I try. I try to put my feelings into the stone . . . stone, not skin. I try. But it's a fight.

LEONARDO. Oh it's a fight, oh yes, oh I know!

MICHELANGELO. Do you? I wonder. Satan lives in my body. Not the one we all draw and paint. With scorched, sweating flesh, with horns and hooves and tail. Not him. The real one. Who's much harder to picture. Yet not to feel. I burn, even in the shadows I burn. Satan's invitations. How can I want these things? Don't know. I have to turn away from him. Turn towards that holy love which, on the cross, opened its arms to me. Why isn't that enough? Why do I ever yearn to turn back to the other one, the evil one?

LEONARDO. Because it's what you say – it's a fight, and it has to be. (*Indicating* VITO.) Why d'you think I took him away with me? He was becoming too interesting . . . he needed fighting – with science. First Experiment. Get to know the object of desire – him – not the chance arrangement of his features and flesh, which happens to be phenomenal – the accident of beauty – get to know him. First Observation. In this case, there's little to know. On the hillside I tried to discuss flying, gliding, the throw of his sling, its angle, its velocity . . . a clue there, surely? . . . but he'd always get bored or just laugh. It was infuriating, but good. First Conclusion (*Touches his head, then crotch*.) . . . As this organ tires of something, so does this one. Second Experiment. I tried to restimulate my interest by dressing him up, painting his face, posing him here and there. Second Observation – nothing worked. Second and Final Conclusion – I was cured.

MICHELANGELO. I think . . . I could get to know him for a hundred years and never be cured.

LEONARDO. No need for a hundred, just fifty will do. Come, picture him then – sitting in the shade of the piazza, the one with all the stories . . . come, picture his features then, the corruption, the decay – draw him in your thoughts . . .

MICHELANGELO. No . . . !

LEONARDO. Yes, crink'd and dry as leather, nose meeting chin like a nutcracker, half-bald, half-blind . . . the decay at work like maggots in his skin . . .

VITO *stirs in his sleep. The drape falls off him.*

. . . Yet look at him now. Had I not cut open bodies, I would swear there is light inside some men, a sure light, a shining.

MICHELANGELO. Yes . . . look. Here.

They indicate different shapes on VITO*'s body.*

LEONARDO. And here.

MICHELANGELO. This line.

LEONARDO. This one.

MICHELANGELO. Yes.

LEONARDO This run of skin, of silk.

MICHELANGELO. Yes. But why?

LEONARDO. Why what?

MICHELANGELO. Why does it make me feel like this? Like an ache.

LEONARDO. Really? I feel it more like a kind of violence. I want to ruin it.

MICHELANGELO. Yes. Yes. Yes! (*Drinks wine.*) But why?

LEONARDO. I don't know.

MICHELANGELO. But you know everything.

LEONARDO. Yes, I do.

They laugh – uneasily.

I know how this muscle folds, making this shape just so, I know about this ridge of bone, this trail of hair, I know man from the inside out. But I don't know why this, the chance arrangement of his features – the accident of beauty – I don't know why this makes us feel like we do, I don't know why it hurts.

MICHELANGELO. The accident of beauty.

LEONARDO. And the difficulty of beauty. For us . . . and for him . . . it is . . .

VITO *stirs in his sleep again, and farts.*

Ah – I think the decay may just have started.

They laugh again. Pause. LEONARDO *covers* VITO *with the drape.*

Let us send him away . . . please.

MICHELANGELO. Why? You're cured. Aren't you? Didn't you say you were cured?

LEONARDO *goes silent.* MICHELANGELO *laughs harshly, and drinks.* LEONARDO *turns to view David.*

LEONARDO. Him too – you should send him away too.

MICHELANGELO. What?

LEONARDO. You should do what Soderini was, in his ignorance, requesting the other day – give it to them now, leave it as it is, let this be it.

MICHELANGELO. But it's not finished . . . !

LEONARDO. Exactly. And that's the other thing about beauty – it's never finished, it's never perfect. The artist has too much time. More time than God or Nature or whatever you want to call the divine spark . . . this rushed at us, threw us together, and rushed on to the next task. How is the artist to capture this rush? It's like a river . . . the water you touch is the last of what has passed, and the first of what is to come . . . and so is it also with Time Present . . . yet how is the artist to capture it, one drop, one instant, and hold it there, suspended, quivering, telling us everything . . . how does he prevent his paint or stone from turning it dry, hard, dead? I don't know. But it's what you've got here, now . . . (*David.*) . . . our eyes finish those places that you haven't, and so there is movement, in us, in him, and . . . it's a miracle.

MICHELANGELO *drinks.* LEONARDO *opens his satchel.*

Y'know, for some time while you've been carving, I've been doing a modest commission for a local silk merchant . . . a portrait of his lady done from the life . . . it's where I was tonight . . .

He takes a painting from a flattish cage, and props it against some marble. We only see it from the back. But MICHELAN-GELO *doesn't, and it's his turn to be amazed.*

MICHELANGELO. This is . . . !

LEONARDO. 'Good'? No, no, a dwarf compared to your Giant, and in truth the work was totally uninteresting at first, the kind we all do for money, with brush in one hand, brains in the other . . . but then . . . well, it was the landscape actually . . . of my own invention, as you can tell . . . a darker, more ancient time . . . and now she has become a . . . well, a darker presence too, more secretive. The reason I show you this is that . . . d'you see . . . I dare not finish it. The husband is growling hard, and yet if I finish it, the secretiveness . . . (*Smiles*.) . . . no, I mustn't even finish this thought . . .

Turning his back sharply, MICHELANGELO *examines the painting's cage.*

MICHELANGELO. Oh I see . . . this protects the fresh colours. Did you invent this? Your brain. Bravo.

LEONARDO *smiles courteously, and starts putting the painting away.*

And how strong is this thing?

LEONARDO. Strong enough.

MICHELANGELO. Let me see . . .

LEONARDO. No . . .

MICHELANGELO. . . . Oh come now . . .

LEONARDO. . . . No, let go, thank you!

MICHELANGELO. . . . Come now, it's only a dwarf as you sway . . . say . . . only a painting . . . (*Staggers away*.) 'S just craft. As my beloved father will tell you. Jus' paintwork, stonework. (*Grabs his heavy mason's mallet and swings it about*.) 'S all right . . . 's just my craft. I break things. I smash, I fight, I hit. And sometimes I make beauty. 'S just my craft . . .

LEONARDO. Stop this!

MICHELANGELO. . . . I break stone into men . . . or men into stone . . . which is which?

He raises the mallet above VITO. LEONARDO *wrestles it from him.*

LEONARDO. No . . . ! Or at least do what you really want.

MICHELANGELO. Which is? Yes?

LEONARDO. What I didn't do. Yet wanted more than . . . Oh, to make me feel that again . . . I hate him, I hate him! (*He weeps; recovers. Pause.*) Look . . . he is not for us, this Ganymede . . . we are neither of us destined to be as pleasured as Jove.

MICHELANGELO. Well . . . it depends which version of the story you . . .

LEONARDO. No, there's only one.

MICHELANGELO. No!

LEONARDO. Yes – an older man stealing and fucking a boy.

MICHELANGELO. Get out of here. Take your stink out of here, your dirt, your black fleas, your pestilence. You make the whole city sick, you and your kind. God rot you – God tear you, tear you! Go – go away!

LEONARDO. I will. (*Indicating* VITO.) And he must too. He . . .

MICHELANGELO. Yes, 'Master'. I have understood, 'Master'. But you have no say in it, 'Master'.

LEONARDO *thinks – then kneels next to* VITO.

LEONARDO. Fly . . . my eagle . . . fly away.

LEONARDO *takes his satchel and exits. Before the door closes,* SALAI *looks in for a long, cold moment.* MICHELANGELO *drinks more wine. The wind rattles the walls.* MICHELANGELO *lurches over to* VITO. *Stretches out one hand.*

MICHELANGELO. Not ready, not ready, not ready . . .

He touches VITO*'s chest, his arm, his belly.* VITO *wakes.* MICHELANGELO *covers his face.*

VITO. Master? I must've . . . (*Struggling to rise.*) Pardon, Master.

MICHELANGELO. Hush. All is well. You're going home.

VITO. Home . . . ?

MICHELANGELO. I don't think Florence is for you.

VITO. D'you know what? I don't think it is, Master.

MICHELANGELO. I'll give you a purse. And gifts for your wife and child. You'll say they're from you. You'll say it all worked well – you made your fortune in the big city. And now you've come home. (VITO *stares at him, amazed.*) We'll arrange it all at first light.

VITO. Master . . . (*Embraces* MICHELANGELO *tightly.*) Thank you, Master, bless you. I will always . . .

The door opens, and SALAI *ushers in the two Savonarola* ACOLYTES. *They see the embrace between the naked* VITO *and half-naked* MICHELANGELO.

ACOLYTE 1 *and* 2. Ohhh.

ACOLYTE 1. The worst.

ACOLYTE 2. The worst, the worst . . .

ACOLYTES 1 *and* 2. . . . The sin of sins!

They slowly come forward. SALAI *watches from the door.*

ACOLYTE 1. What does the holy one say?

ACOLYTE 2. God's Jaws, God's Jaws.

ACOLYTE 1. This city is become . . .

ACOLYTE 2. The Second Sodoma . . .

ACOLYTE 1. And he who lies with meat . . .

ACOLYTE 2. Boy meat . . .

ACOLYTE 1. Boy meat with eyes . . .

ACOLYTE 2. Meat with eyes, meat with eyes . . .

ACOLYTE 1. He must hurt, hurt . . .

ACOLYTES 1 *and* 2. Hurt, hurt, hurt . . . !

They pick up pieces of marble. ACOLYTE 2 *aims at*
MICHELANGELO.

ACOLYTE 1. No . . . the idol.

ACOLYTE 2. The idol?

ACOLYTE 1. To hurt the man, hurt his idol.

ACOLYTE 2. His naked idol . . .

They hurl pieces of marble at David's genitals.

ACOLYTE 1 *and* 2. Hurt, hurt, hurt . . . !

MICHELANGELO *is rigid with horror. But the missiles have
done no damage. The* ACOLYTES *pick up larger chunks:*

Hurt, hurt, hurt . . . !

Before they can throw, VITO *leaps in front of the statue.*

VITO. Nay, you shall not . . . !

The ACOLYTES *hesitate, then look at one another.*

ACOLYTE 1. Or him.

ACOLYTE 2. The boy meat!

ACOLYTES 1 *and* 2. Hurt, hurt, hurt . . . !

They start stoning VITO *with pieces of marble. He runs. They
pursue, scooping up ammunition as they go, and chanting
prayers.* VITO *reaches the door.* SALAI *shuts it tight.* VITO
runs again. The ACOLYTES *herd him into a back corner of
the yard, and unleash a storm of stones. Then they suddenly
start to retreat.* VITO*'s voice is heard from the shadows.*

VITO. Here – the Scorpion – here – bite on the Scorpion!

VITO *whirls back into view, armed with his Scorpion, his
sling, firing marble stones. The* ACOLYTES *charge to the
door.*

(*Aiming at* SALAI.) You too – Little Devil – here – taste the
Scorpion!

SALAI *is struck – yelping, he flees with the* ACOLYTES. VITO *slams the door behind them.*

I am Vito Barattini of Carrara. And nobody does that to me!

VITO *stands, panting.* MICHELANGELO *stares, amazed. Blackout. The cast assemble and sing a Latin version of Psalm 18 (Verse 10). 'And he rode upon a cherub and did fly . . . '*

Scene Twelve

. . . As the song finishes, we see a yellow dawn. The yard is empty – David is gone. MICHELANGELO *enters, gazing at something out-front. He's no longer coated in marble mud, but still scruffy.* SPINI, PANDOLFINI, *and* LODOVICO *arrive, all gazing out-front. A huge shadow starts to appear on one side: the silhouette of the finished statue as the sun rises behind it.* WORKMEN *cross with ropes and logs.* LEONARDO *arrives with* SALAI *and* ENTOURAGE.

LEONARDO (*staring up at David; to* MICHELANGELO).
D'you know . . . I seek two things, two things chiefly, and then my spirit will be free . . . how to explain beauty . . . how to achieve flight. And you may just have solved both. It's simply a gift. A gift above all others. (MICHELANGELO *nods, giving gruff thanks.*) Though I still think it was better unfinished.

They laugh, but neither is at ease. MACHIAVELLI *arrives.*

LEONARDO *and* MICHELANGELO (*bowing*). Secretary.

MACHIAVELLI. Worthy Masters. (*Looking up at David.*) Oh . . . magnificent, bravo! How will Florence ever thank you?

LEONARDO. You could try giving him more money.

They all laugh – again uneasily. MACHIAVELLI *indicates the statue.*

MACHIAVELLI. So, tell me, how exactly will this work – the transport?

MICHELANGELO. We've hoisted him onto that platform, Secretary. It's on greased beams. And now we'll roll him through the streets.

MACHIAVELLI. And you are content with his placing?

MICHELANGELO. His placing is an honour, Secretary.

MACHIAVELLI. I'm pleased you think so. He will stand on the Ringhiera, outside the Palazzo Vecchio, at the doors of government itself, with his face and his frown turned southwards, towards Rome, with its ferocious Borgias and its exiled Medicis. He will warn all to stay away. He will be a new lion, a new symbol of Florence.

LEONARDO. Ah, and I remember when he was just a statue, just an adornment for the Duomo.

MACHIAVELLI (*ignoring* LEONARDO; *speaking to* MICHELANGELO). And you are content also with the . . . ehrm . . . ?

A huge brass fig leaf is carried across the stage by the WORKMEN.

MICHELANGELO. No – I'm not at all content with that, I'm . . . !

MACHIAVELLI. Oh it's just for now, worthy Master, trust us, please. The impact of the Giant on our citizens is going to be so tremendous, we just felt they need a little time before also absorbing the shock of your uncircumcised Hebrew.

MICHELANGELO (*unamused*). Pray pardon, Secretary, but I must . . .

He exits.

LEONARDO. Pardon me too, Secretary – pray pardon for the Arno.

MACHIAVELLI. Hmn? Ah – 'Pardon for the Arno' – well put!

LEONARDO. I haven't seen you to say how . . .

MACHIAVELLI (*with a cold smile*). Oh no, no, I just found it hilarious – ranks of soldiers knee-deep in mud – hilarious. No, no, it was Soderini who was upset, not me. But as we say of him in the Signoria . . .

LEONARDO. . . . Sod Soderini.

MACHIAVELLI (*hesitates – this joke is his*). . . . I was actually going to say the man is so indecisive, it was a relief to see him roused. As least he knew what he thought about this – 'We tried to move a river and it didn't work – what a surprise!'

LEONARDO (*quietly*). It could've worked . . . the machinery wasn't up to it.

MACHIAVELLI. Ah well, no doubt you'll please him again. How's the mural coming along, the 'Battle'?

LEONARDO. Yes, good, thank you.

MACHIAVELLI. Because a friend of mine came to spy on you – do forgive him – and he thought there was some slippage of the colours.

LEONARDO. It's all solved now.

MACHIAVELLI. Good. Because we've also heard the regrettable news about your mural in the Milan convent – the mould – the colours slipping again.

LEONARDO (*trying to laugh*). Oh, that restless work . . . ! I was attempting something new, oil and varnish instead of fresco, and it didn't . . .

MACHIAVELLI. Ah me, dear me . . . whether river-moving machinery or wall-painting materials . . . nothing's ever quite right. A word of advice, if I may. Confess these things to me by all means, we've shared many indiscretions, but do be wary of saying them abroad. We don't want you developing a reputation as that unfortunate workman of legend, the one who blames his tools.

LEONARDO (*bowing his head*). Secretary.

MACHIAVELLI. You are a Master of so many things. Don't add Failure to your list.

LEONARDO (*passionately*). One tries not to, Secretary, but to every artist . . . Creation is his firstborn, and Failure his bastard child. It dogs him, this unwanted thing, it is at his heels, it is his shadow. He does what he can to stay ahead.

MACHIAVELLI. And you speak as a bastard child yourself, do you not?

LEONARDO *goes silent*.

Perhaps he is closer to your heart – the bastard one. This is where we are so different. In government there is no such thing as Failure. It doesn't exist. There is only Success, and when there is no Success, there is talk of Success, of past Success, future Success, Success in Heaven or in the history books. And hence we never have to fear your little bastard, your little F-word. (*As* MICHELANGELO *passes, carrying rope*.) Oh, and has anyone mentioned this yet? We're giving him the space next to you – in the council hall – the other 'Battle' scene.

LEONARDO. But . . . can he paint? (*Silence*.) No, no one's mentioned it.

MACHIAVELLI. Just think – two great 'Battles' side by side. Someone was saying the other day – it may even have been me – we're going to get three 'Battles' for the price of two. The two 'Battle' scenes, and the battle of the artists. This statue will cause a sensation. Then, before the city draws breath, we will give them something even greater. The Battle of David and Goliath – but for real, and – which is which?

LEONARDO. I had no idea the Colosseum was still operational, the Games still thriving.

MACHIAVELLI. Oh yes. It's our natural human instinct to seek excitement – especially in the Arts, and in Government.

LEONARDO. Excitement . . . and some blood.

MACHIAVELLI. Without blood there's no excitement. Oh look . . . !

The Giant has started moving, with a huge grinding noise. During the rest of the scene, its colossal shadow will slowly pass over the onlookers like an eclipse.

(*To* MICHELANGELO.) Good, everything seems to be proceeding well, so I'll greet you at the other end. How long do they think . . . ?

MICHELANGELO. Up to five days, Secretary.

MACHIAVELLI. Five days – and I can walk it in five minutes! Well, well, some of us are born to be gigantic warriors, some puny secretaries, and both destinies offer certain advantages. Right, good, excellent, see you in five days then . . .

MACHIAVELLI exits.

LEONARDO (*to* MICHELANGELO). My salutations on your new commission . . . I think it's an excellent thing . . . we're going to be working side by side for a long time, with much to talk of, much to learn . . . each from the other.

MICHELANGELO doesn't respond. They gaze up at David.

Did you send him home, by the way, as we discussed?

MICHELANGELO. I did.

LEONARDO. Did he reach there safely, do we know?

MICHELANGELO. We don't.

LEONARDO. He can't write, so I suppose we'll never . . . (*Pause.*) Do you miss him?

MICHELANGELO. No. Do you?

LEONARDO (*after a beat*). No.

They part – LEONARDO *to his* ENTOURAGE. *He embraces* SALAI.

Come, my creature, my bat, my devil, my ningle . . .

SALAI. Come, my darla, my dilling, my oyster . . .

They laugh and exit. MICHELANGELO *moves to* LODOVICO.

MICHELANGELO. I'm going to walk along with the Giant, Father. Will you walk with me? I would so . . .

SPINI. You're his father . . . ?!

PANDOLFINI. Ah, Saint Giovanni – bravo – great honour on your name!

LODOVICO. Thank you – but my name, Buonarroti, is, as you must know, already a very distinguished one . . .

SPINI. Ah but this, this . . . ! (*David*.) Sacred Jesus, you must be proud!

LODOVICO. Well, I don't really know much about stonework.

SPINI *and* PANDOLFINI *are dumbstruck. They exit.*

MICHELANGELO (*to* LODOVICO). Will you walk with me . . . ?

LODOVICO. I'd like to, I would . . . it's just that I must go to the butcher . . . the stupid man is getting incensed over, I don't know, some bills he says we haven't . . .

MICHELANGELO. Yes, yes.

He gives LODOVICO *money.* LODOVICO *accepts in his usual, resentful way, then exits.* MICHELANGELO *stands alone, with the shadow of David slowly passing over him. A figure appears at the back. He and* MICHELANGELO *don't seem to see one another.* MICHELANGELO *exits.*

Epilogue

David's shadow clears over the figure – it's OLD VITO.

OLD VITO. That then is my story. And if any doubt it, this is what we say in the mountains – a marble block is only beautiful when you take some of it away – a story is only beautiful when you add something to it. (*Guffaws*.) So aye . . . I met them, those giants, I met them, I knew them, and then I went home to Carrara. And oh it was good, d'you know, to be with my people again. My Maria and my little Flavia, who wasn't so little no more . . . (*Whistles, clicks tongue*.) And so we grew, we all grew, we grew old, and we sat on our mountain, with its echoes and its big, big view. And somewhere over there . . . there lay the city. But it's only like a field, y'know, only like the seasons, only going round and round too. And as time went by, we heard the news . . .

The lone voice starts singing. Figures cross the stage from different directions, looking up at David. SODERINI *is first to be seen:*

The Gonfaloniere for Life – he only lasted ten years, ey?

MACHIAVELLI *is seen.*

The Secretary, he was thrown into prison, put to torture. Why? 'Cause the old dukes, the Medicis, they came back to rule.

The Savonarola ACOLYTES *are seen.*

And those mad ones – they were right – God's Jaws came back too. God's Jaws started talking again. His books, his teachings. People following again.

LEONARDO *is seen.*

Him – him I never saw again. And I'm sorry about that. I miss him. I loved him. (*Shrugs.*) But . . . well, he wasn't a man of luck. He spoiled the 'Battle' painting. Wrong materials again, colours running off the wall, the whole thing just a . . . ffff! Then he left Florence, and . . . well, I don't know what happened to him then. As for the other one, my Master . . .

MICHELANGELO *is seen.*

. . . He never even started his 'Battle' painting. Just did the cartoon, then left Florence too, for other work. So the big Battle of the Artists, this never happened – the David and Goliath battle – and which one is which. But I did see him again. 'Course I did – he kept coming to Carrara for his marble. I saw him, but he didn't really see me. I mean, like, when we passed in the streets or the quarries, he'd nod, but, d'you know, as to a stranger . . . and then, off he'd go, with that look, like he's carrying all the shame of the world inside him.

He looks up at David.

And as for him . . . even as the giant set off walking that day, folk were starting to say, this statue is not just the best in Italy, but the whole world. Think of that. And it's me. Just think! (*Laughs.*) But, nay, nay – don't take my word for it. Go look. In his right hand . . . on the handle of the sling. Go look what my Master carved on the handle. One letter. 'V.' Vito. Vito Barattini of Carrara. (*Laughs.*) These great ones, these giants, they come, they go, to Heaven and to Hell. But one person in my story, he lives on. Carrara marble is made to last, ey? 'V' . . .

He reaches for young VITO, *who comes on and takes his hand.*

VITO. 'V' . . . on and on . . .

OLD VITO. Through the years, the ages, all the way to the end of time . . .

VITO. 'V', 'V', 'V' . . .

OLD VITO. It's what was promised . . .

VITO. Like eagles and angels . . .

TOGETHER. We can fly.

The two VITOS *reach up. The lone voice sings. The Giant exits.*

Blackout.

The End.

A Nick Hern Book

The Giant first published in Great Britain in 2007 as a paperback original by Nick Hern Books Limited, 14 Larden Road, London W3 7ST, in association with Hampstead Theatre

Cover image: www.n9design.com
Cover design: Ned Hoste, 2H

Typeset by Nick Hern Books, London
Printed and bound in Great Britain by CPI Bookmarque, Croydon, Surrey

A CIP catalogue record for this book is available from the British Library

ISBN 978 1 85459 588 1